Six Feet Tall, Three Feet Short

Outlook on Life, A Collection of Reflections from a Wheelchair

Moses Bilsky

Edited and Designed by Jorie Bilsky McCarthy

AuthorHouse™
1663 Liberty Drive
Bloomington, IN 47403
www.authorhouse.com
Phone: 1-800-839-8640

©2011 Moses Bilsky. All rights reserved.

No part of this book may be reproduced, stored in a retrieval system, or transmitted by any means without the written permission of the author.

First published by AuthorHouse   01/24/2011

ISBN: 978-1-4567-1304-1 (sc)
ISBN: 978-1-4567-1306-5 (hc)
ISBN: 978-1-4567-1305-8 (sc)

Library of Congress Control Number: 2010918452

Printed in the United States of America

Any people depicted in stock imagery provided by Thinkstock are models, and such images are being used for illustrative purposes only. Certain stock imagery © Thinkstock.

This book is printed on acid-free paper.

Because of the dynamic nature of the Internet, any Web addresses or links contained in this book may have changed since publication and may no longer be valid. The views expressed in this work are solely those of the author and do not necessarily reflect the views of the publisher, and the publisher hereby disclaims any responsibility for them.

About the Author

Moses (Moe) Bilsky was born in 1923 Ottawa Canada and moved to the United States when he was twelve. Residing in Kentucky through his youth, he found a love of horses; a passion for the "Art's" became an accomplished pianist, and devoted Son to his Mother and Father. After serving in World War II as a tank driver under General George Patton, he returned to the States to finish his education earning a LLB and his JD. Throughout his career he mastered several industries including a motorcycle dealership, (his favorite - as his dress was similar to that of riding a horse, head to toe leather and riding free in the wind), investment banking, real estate and textiles/furniture.

He met Marcia, the love of his life in 1953 and moved to Chicago to raise a family. He is a devoted husband and father and shares his love, courage and passion for life with his wife and three children. He has always been a positive and encouraging influence in their lives.

Reflections from a Stroke Survivor

Dedication I

To Marcia;

There is no flower or jewel to equal the beauty I see in you every day. Were it in my power, I would walk beside you into eternity, and wish, that moment in life and time was forever.

Dedication II

These writings are dedicated to our children who in the flash of an eye, were there when needed.

Not expecting to see such a respectful change, they matured instantaneously. Their Mother and I, no longer at the strong helm, were safe, and grateful to be surrounded by such support.

The daughter in Realty Management, the daughter in California Corporate Purchasing, and the Glass Designer extraordinaire son, stood silent and strong, and accomplished on a 24/7 bases, independence, reliability, and family loyalty.

We didn't raise them well, we loved them well.

Forward A - I Don't Think It Matters

Happy or sad – rich or poor – of any color or religion - crown prince or cabdriver – old or young - champion - valedictorian – blind or deaf - When a Stroke Hits, You're Hit.

What is important is continuing to exist as best as possible. Treatment, attitude, wanting to improve, patience, time, all combinations toward a common goal. Even a finger twitch can be exciting.

Forward B

Don't stop trying to be what you want to be – better today than yesterday. Only you will know if there is a power greater than your imagination.

Table of Contents

Chapter I - 911 The Floor Hit Me   1

Chapter II – Gurney To Oblivion   2

Chapter III – Strike One - You're Out 8 Days   3

Chapter IV - Who Me? Why!   4

Chapter V - Marissa - Wow   5

Chapter VI - Rollover - Relax   6

Chapter VII - You Listen. I'll Cry.   7

Chapter VIII – Hang Me Up? What For?   9

Chapter IX - It Won't Bend   10

Chapter X – Slide What? Where?   11

Chapter XI - Join The Group   12

Chapter XII - 10 Things I Know For Sure   13

Chapter XIII - Bend Over - Fall Over   16

Chapter XIV - Safe At Last?   17

Chapter XV - Most Exciting Experience - I Don't Remember   18

Chapter XVI - Celebrate The Obvious   19

Chapter XVII – Butterflies are Free   20

PART TWO OR THE SECOND PART OF
THE LONG HAUL BACK

Chapter I– And All The While I Wondered   21

Chapter II – Why Wait – It's My Weight   22

Chapter III – Today Is Today   24

Chapter IV – Chicago Is - - - -   27

Chapter V – Why So Picky?   28

Chapter VI – It's What – Not When   29

Chapter VII – Sex – Shall We Talk?   30

Chapter VIII – Keep In Mind The Following   31

It @ Four am	37
Ode To Whomever	37
Don't Tell My Doctor	38
A Tear Because	39
I Know We Can	40
Hold On – Custer!	42
Cut It Fair	43
I've Got The World	44
I Will If You Will	45
My Love	46
Second Chance?	48
Once In Far Off Memory	49
A Word For "Well"	50
The Black Knight	51
Rhythms	52
Another Woman	53
Home	54
Moonlight	55
Soul Keeper	58
Life Is A Pill	59
Thinking To Write About	60
I Dun It Forbidden Fruit!	61
Full – Half - Empty	62
Luck	63
Cards	63
Why?	64
Strut On	65
What You Don't See – Is What You Get	66
Good Bye With Love	67
Tired? Not Me.	68
A Brother Lost	69

No Time Out	70
No Response	70
Still Time Left	71
A Necessary Cut	72
Mix And Match	73
Imagination	74
Anything Is Possible	75
New Moon	76
It's Now Or Never	78
Funny?	79
A New Chance	80
We Need	80
Advise	82
A Pipe Dream	84
Ring That Bell	85
Fun Thoughts	86
Time	87
Doctor	88
An Old Poke	90
In The River	91
What If	92
A View From A Seat Between Wheels	93
A Purpose For An Active Mind	94
Who Are You?	96
Think Now	97
Remembering	98
A Special Thought	99
A 6 Minute Thought –	100
The Silliness Of Me	101
Fantasy	102
And Then There Is Me	104

Sub – Zero	105
Thanks Dad	106
Legacy	107
Can You Hear Me	108
Lost Feeling	109
Total Nonsense	110
Spider	111
A Personal Moment	112
A Restless Mind	113
Dates Remembered	114
Inbetween	124
Tomorrow's Order	126
Above And Beyond	127
No – Nevermind – I'll Just Sit Here Alone And Cry	128
Be It Known	129
Reflections Of A Tired Mind	130
An Irresistible Thought – From An Irresponsible Mind.	130
Woodchuck In The Willow	131
Life	132
A.M. – Maybe?	133
"Lilly Lovely"	134
Personal Challenge	135
Midnight Roamer	136
Just In Time – A Rhyme	137
Someone	138
Life Is A Gamble	139
Thoughts Before Thinking	140
Thoughts – After Thinking	141
Meaningful Words	142
Again – Again And Again	143
Quick – Say	145

It's Important	146
Four Seasons	146
Just Nonsence	147
It's Okay	148
A True Story? Maybe	150
Humpty Dumpty	151
Thoughts	152
Five	152
Easy As Pie	153
Fight	154
Written	155
Fiction & Facts, From Moe's Almanac	156
I Watch	156
I Would If I Could	157
Tomorrow	158
I Win	159
Now	160
Again - ? – !	161
Humpty Dumpty Ii	162
He Said, You Said, I Said	163
The Best	164
That's It	166
Ah! What's Up Doc?	167
All Together Now	168
Nightmares	169
A Crying Smile	170
Wow – And Then – Wow	172
Barefoot Beggar	175
It Takes More Than Effort	176
Don't Expect A Miracle	177
With Apology To Cole Porter	178

Involved	180
Just A Thought One Night	181
Doing Vs. Thinking	182
Wheelchair	183
All's Well	186
Satisfaction	187
Lucky	189
It's Different Down Here	190
Safety Abounds	192

100 PAGES FOR ALL AGES

A lesson taught – Cannot be bought.

If you Believe – You can achieve.

Show you care – Please share.

If the shoe fits – you're lucky.

You don't need to be Smart – To Fart.

THE UNQUENCHABLE THIRST

It's the brightness of togetherness that lights the dark path of future loneliness – and the road continues on the edge of courage. Faith is the leader, and with hope, our will and desire, prove to be adequate support.

And so I wanted to tell a story – meaningful, with purpose and humor. From sketches on a little pad – through three corrective attempts – three proofing's – One hundred plus printed handouts – finally someone noticed, and now, after fifteen months from the beginning –

I'm proud to present:

> "Six Feet Tall – Three Feet Short"

Enjoy – Think – Share – and count your blessings.

"M.B."

Chapter I - 911 The Floor Hit Me

When you least expect the unexpected - WOW, it happens. In good health, shaving in the bathroom, and whistling about 5:00 P.M. – getting ready to take my wife out to dinner, I felt a tremor in my right knee. Then it spread, first my foot – my leg tightened – my thigh felt numb. I couldn't hold myself up. I grabbed the sink. I started to slide backwards. My shoulder pushed the shower glass panel. Because we kept the shower door held ajar for the dog. I fell backwards into the shower – my back, pressing against the threshold, I lay backwards into the shower. My wife being near by, hearing my call, (really a scream) came running. "Call 911" - I was barely audible. Within 10 minutes, our apartment was buzzing.

Doors opening, telephones busy, heavily coated, and booted firemen. I thought of my father's favorite definition of formaldehyde. "From all da hiding places came the Indians." As I said, 'the apartment was buzzing'.

Chapter II – Gurney To Oblivion

Can you hear me? I responded, "YES". I heard "all together on the count of" ----- it faded out. But I felt being picked up and my chin was no longer forced into my chest. The cart manipulated around corners - I saw my wife near me - I realized the ceiling Lobby lights were to bright - I felt the cool night air - I saw my son and asked where Marcia was - assured – the ambulance was moving and I loved the sound of the siren – that's it. Lights out and oblivion set in.

Chapter III – Strike One - You're Out 8 Days

When strike one is called on the Cubs – they still have two more attempts at survival. My strike one kept me out of the conscious game for the following eight days. Not lucid what so ever, I am told I wanted the ceiling lights realigned in order – the television moved to the other corner, the bed turned to the windows, and the guest lounge chair pushed away, and the doctor telling someone he had a circus going on in the room.

But evidently, medication, attention and love brought me back to the land of the living, and I became aware of being back on a gurney, and being pushed through long tunnels to I know not where.

But the where proved to be the Rehab Institute of Chicago at N.W., a safe haven indeed! Ending the wheeled trip in a huge room for 4 beds, I was the only patient. Window by the lake, my bed by the window, I saw my family gathered, and their smiles enticed me to smile back.

Now if I can only get out of bed and go home.

Chapter IV - Who Me? Why!

So – realization of facts finally have to be faced. Great as I thought I was – invincible, daredevil, speed artist, and champion of all, I've had a stroke. Right side paralysis – toes to ear, limb upon limb, muscle connected to muscle nothing worked. Couldn't even turn from back to side.

How is this possible? Biceps - Quads – Didn't even know what they were. Overextended use – no way. Strictly, muscles used for piano, dancing, cocktails, and wife holding – now nothing coordinated with my thinking. I was told maybe a clogged artery on the left side of my throat. Take my word for it - Don't get one – Very debilitating.

Chapter V - Marissa - Wow

A shocking revelation when one is lying in bed and realizing you can't get up is the thought of one's bathroom responsibilities. Toilets, teeth, hand washing - Hey! What about a shower? I was numbered even - I new I wasn't odd?? Well, let me tell you. R.I. has a system and personnel with the know-how. Pushing into the room by your attendant is a giant contraption that is capable of dock loading a ship in a New York Harbor. They call it Marissa – I don't know why, but it gets the job done. Rolling to the side, a tarp like material is tucked under you. Reversing a hold on the opposite bedside, suddenly the four corners are hooked up like a meat scale, and you're cranked up ready for shipment. This is on an even day. Can you imagine what happens on an odd day?

And off you go into the shower. The WOW part comes when you get wet, a soaped up washcloth slides wherever possible, and you begin to feel half human. My attendant with complete gentleness gets me back into bed – dries me off – and says "How's that?"

Feeling human once more, I realize I made progress from yesterday, I know there is hope. A prayer might help right now - I Prayed.

Chapter VI - Rollover - Relax

Learning to roll over from side to side, trying to shift your body weight, learning the buttons on the bedside – up, down, head, feet, knees, call buttons, lights, TV, - Your not at home – But your getting acclimated to current accommodations.

If body functions are to be active, the equipment for same is there and if you cannot handle the bed pan, the staff is gentle, accommodating, non-accusatory and efficient, - relax, lucky to be alive. Take one step at a time – look forward to the next step.

Chapter VII - You Listen. I'll Cry.

Posted on the door of my room was tomorrow's schedule - O.T. - 9:00 a.m. seems very early to me. But if someone gets me started for the day, I'll see what O.T. stands for. A moment of thought and I realized its occupational therapy. At 9:00 a.m. I don't know if my breakfast will be settled – If I can get into my shorts, shoes, shirt – but I must try.

O.T. is group participation. To me that's an immediate turn off. But I have to be there if I am to be considered an R.I. patient. I needed them more than they need me. Wheeling down to the large gathering room, I joined a table of unpleasantness. Eight is not just a number, but also a collection of illness far greater than mine – I thought. But the therapist was most kind. He directed me to an open spot around the table. I was not comfortable. After we mentioned each name, I asked to be called Moe, Mr. Bilsky was my father and grandfather.

So, we all had to do and choose something. Not me, I'm a pianist extraordinaire. I'll just watch.

"Moe, so as not to embarrass the group, please join us for a few exercises, neck muscles – arm raises - etc." "Tomorrow, we will bring a keyboard and you can play."

Great, I began to brag about my entertainment abilities, asking each member of the group "What would you like to hear?" I know that - I can play that" – This get together won't be so bad after all. Skipping through the rest of the day I was anxious to show off to all the next morning.

Around the table – there we were – each doing tasks of their choosing and laboring to do so. And then someone put a two-octave keyboard in front of me. Great – I again asked each patient if they remembered their request – some did, some didn't. The mind is a bit quirky after a stroke. "Moe – time to show off" they turned the keyboard on and I positioned my wheel

Moses Bilsky

chair. And then it happened. My right hand, sitting on my right thigh, wouldn't come up to the table – let alone touch the keyboard. Completely unnerved I immediately broke down and cried uncontrollably.

Through my tears, and hearing voices saying, "don't worry", and "It's OK" my mind wandered back 60 years. And I remembered as a tank driver in WWII, I would be called upon by the Chaplin or Rabbi to drive to a certain location where emergency prayers were being said. And I would provide background music in the field on a small foot pump organ. I always played Amazing Grace.

And with this vision in mind my left hand picked up my right arm and placed it in position to the keyboard. With one finger, I correctly hit the beginning note of Amazing Grace, and followed through with the correct melody – in perfect time.

I was so proud. I stopped crying – looked at each of my fellow patients, who's eyes had now teared, and I knew for sure, I was playing the greatest concert in my life – to the most appreciative and listening audience I had ever had.

I knew at that moment I would recover enough to eventually get back home to my loving wife of 50 years.

I am truly blessed. And I now have a completely different view of the people less fortunate than I and the world around me.

Chapter VIII – Hang Me Up? What For?

You don't volunteer for physical therapy. You're assigned, listed, scheduled, and expected to show up on time.

So, I'm going down the hallway and I talked to myself - "P.T." My GOD – do they know I'm 80 years old – that my bones and muscles ain't what they use to be? Will they take into account I've had a hernia, a plastic aorta from head to toe, colon cancer, spinal stenosis, an arthritic spine and all extremities laden with big and little spots of arthritis?

So what! I was told to slide or "transfer" as the therapist called it to the padded worktable or bed. It could accommodate 4 patients. Actually like sardines packed head to toe. I followed instructions and was amazed to realize my right leg was now in a sling, hooked to the ceiling grillwork. Rising up on one elbow, I could see the purpose. My leg could swing back and forth effortlessly – except I had to think about what I was doing – and count to 12 – that's so easy. But everyone around me is counting also – it's not easy to remember where you are number wise, when everyone else is at a different number. So with the hand nearest to the work pad on which I lay, I used my fingers – one, two, three, four, five, and back one, two, three, four, five and them my other hand handled the eleven and twelve. Keeping fingers busy and the order of movement – little to thumb and thumb to little, blocked out the sound of everyone counting. It worked for me.

Chapter IX - It Won't Bend

It's amazing what a therapist can accomplish, with a scared old patient, who will acquiesce to kindness and tenderness. It was never do it or else. "Let's try" seemed to create a simple path to "there – I knew you could."

I overworked the expression "It ain't easy being green" – Not the color but reference to being new and what was being done for me – to get me on the road to recovery. When tired or anxious I looked at the clocks – clocks are everywhere – all halls, all rooms. I liked 12 to 1:30 the best. It meant back to my room, bathroom, and somewhat of a lunch at a table in my room. Each day, my guest of honor, my wife. Talk about comfort food – this for me, was real personal comfort.

Chapter X – Slide What? Where?

Slip/sliding away. Sometimes my shorts didn't allow my crotch to slip if I was sliding – and if the board (really a bridge to transportation) wasn't in the correct position - I couldn't slip or slide – and if my shorts twisted at that point, I caught my breath but my crotch couldn't breathe at all.

Better learn this procedure early, since it is an escape route to more interesting routines.

In the exercise area you get to shift from chair to table, work out new maneuverable routines, and get back to the mobility chair of life. Once you've mastered it, life becomes much more simplified.

Chapter XI - Join The Group

I previously mentioned group therapy, and how thoroughly devastated I was to be just one in the crowd, with similar problems.

I was lucky – I could talk, focus, listen, and do some of the tasks assigned. Not necessarily to my liking, but creating a movement needed for healing an ailing muscle. So I did what all at my table did – arms up, arms down, neck left, neck right, head up and left, head down and right.

I really felt foolish – but from the corner of my eye I saw our therapist leading us on and doing the same thing. My ego wouldn't let him do better than me, so I kept even with him. And when he stopped, and the count stopped, I did one more, just to know that I could. Now I could tell my wife how well I was progressing.

Chapter XII - 10 Things I Know For Sure

A) When little, it seems as though I couldn't do or think anything off course, with which to cause trouble, or get into trouble. And the major reason was that my mother had eyes in the back of her head. I couldn't see them, but they were there.

Lucky me - I inherited the same talent once I became confined and attached to my wheel chair. If the floor was smooth, and the hallway long and straight, going forward as fast as I could coddle the wheels – tightening a grip on a wheel could spin you 180 degrees in an instant, and with the push of one foot, propel you down the hall to your destination far faster than going forward.

Dangerous – yes, speedy – especially – especially if you are headed to the bathroom. So, "U" turns are permitted with caution, especially when in a hurry.

B) You have to make the most out of every moment. Calm yourself by believing you can, even if you can't. Being able to deal with what your dealt makes you realize the alternative might be worse.

C) Where is it written or what doctor says your nights are destined to be sleepless. And who dictates to you that each day forward, has to be more worrisome than the previous one.

If you work hard and concentrate on each minute, the big hand swings past the little hand and the hours diminish the time to wonder – what's next?

D) A brave front has its purpose – even though the system has instantaneous set backs that have you crying on the inside. I always smiled to myself that although I had dry eyes, most of the time from sitting in my wheel chair, I had a wet or perspiring crotch.

I'd laugh out loud when I would think of a book title that would really sell - "DRY EYES - WET CROTCH". Would they actually print it? What would it look like in a bookstore window display? Would it look well and

Moses Bilsky

not sell or just the reverse? I think I'm too far out of the norm to be an author – I'll just think up titles for chapters.

E) Have you ever thought how much safer spoons are than forks? I found out when I realized that a fork in my right hand could not align directly toward my mouth when my wrist could not gracefully manipulate a direct twist to my face.

If the item was not stabbed through, it would fall – generally on my shirt or pants. The food was lost, the clothes had to be laundered, and if it happened enough times, I stayed hungry.
So, spoons became my weapon of choice. Even shaky hands could still manage to shovel a little nourishment down the old hungry gullet.

F) If it weren't for doorknobs or door handles I would be still outside in some hall or passage way. Even when open, the doorknob was like a greeting from a friendly hand. I could hold on, pull my wheel chair through or over the floor frame. If you can't hit the exact middle of the open area, watch out for bruised knuckles on either hand.

G) 18" is only a foot and a half. But it's 18" too far to turn on the faucet in the sink. My knees and wheels hit the cupboard underneath, and I have to partially stand to turn on the water - and then fill the sink in order to immerse my hands in the water.

H) It's much easier to get into a swimming pool than get out. The rule of "Good foot up – Bad foot down" on steps is great, providing you don't slip, fall or drown before you enjoy water therapy. And you will be surprised that it holds true for bathtubs. I was able to get in – but it took a 1/2-hour to get out, with the aid of two helpers and all 6 of our hands. Now I'm just happy in the shower.

I) Think ahead – no matter where you go there are obstacles. Can you fit through doors; are there steps, corners, obstacles in store aisles, bells for alarm or to summons help – rugs – curbs – is an item reachable, are all items of required use available?

J) On the street you need peripheral vision – nobody has it, but you need it. The crowd always seems to cross in front of you, never behind. How fast do the lights change at the corner – better to be sure and wait. Realize

Six Feet Tall, Three Feet Short

that if you're freewheeling, you're faster than the average daydreaming walker, or one pushing a baby stroller. Show courtesy even though you don't always get it.

Chapter XIII - Bend Over - Fall Over

While in training – I like to think of it as training to being independent rather than Rehab. I always had a question pop into my mind. I wouldn't hear the pop, but I questioned about falling – from bed, from wheel chair, from commode or from anywhere.

I shouldn't have asked, since in a few moments, spread before me were a series of padded mats all around my wheel chair.

Told to "Bend over", I tried. "Further, you'll be okay" I heard 3 therapists say in unison. So lowering my head and shoulders to my knees, you bet, - they were right, I fell out of the chair and onto the mat in a very ridiculous shape and a position of helplessness.

Now came the lesson. Falling was easy – recovering is the problem. I thought all I would have to do is push up with my arms; get to my knees and pull up on the chair. I said I thought that's what I had to do. No idea, thought, or encouragement was helpful. I tried, and tried again – finally the three therapists lifted me up and positioned me back in my chair.

Lesson learned – I needed help. I was not strong enough physically or mentally to handle the problem, I cried unnecessarily because I was safe – and most of all – don't fall.

Chapter XIV - Safe At Last?

There is really no safe haven after a stroke has struck. Just the assurance that once back home, the attention you receive is loving, constant, and has no bounds.

With professional guidance, and surrounded by the familiar, your day is less worrisome, and the nights are more restful.

If you're pulling on something, holding onto anything, being supported by it, or resting on it, be sure first, it won't move, shift or shake. That's how accidents happen.

I always knew that "bribery brings or gets attention". Candy and nuts in the hospital and Rehab Center gives rise to "How are you feeling Mr. Bilsky" or "Can I get you anything before I go off duty?" In most cases, it also included having a snack or satisfying a sweet tooth and by the time I was released and ready to go home, I had formed some strong opinions.

In the kindest way I thought of the following definitions:

Nurses;
15% Comfort
10% Sympathy
75% Chocolate

And then as for the Doctors;
50% Diagnostic
50% Billing

Chapter XV - Most Exciting Experience - I Don't Remember

Oh yes; now I do – I can sum it up in four sentences:
Seeing daylight,
Being awake,
Sleeping instead of being unconscious,
Talking,
Listening,
Seeing family,
Breathing,
Treated well,
Watching Peregrine Falcons fly,
Turning over,
Eating,
Scratching,
Learning to move,
Brushing my teeth by moving my head, not the toothbrush.

Did I mention waking up and breathing?
And holding my wife's hand,
Answering the telephone,
Picking my nose with either hand,
And by the way, did I emphasize waking up each morning and breathing?

By GOD, There is a GOD – and prayers being answered, and most important, did I mention my wife of 50 years? I'm not just lucky, I'm blessed.

Chapter XVI - Celebrate The Obvious

1. Daylight (It comes with regularity);
2. Nighttime (Time to relax, contemplate and pray for thanks for the coming of tomorrow);
3. A deep breath;

Luckily to purify the system, how it reaches everywhere and gives purpose for the next one, the next day, week, month, year and life. Live strong and with purpose – the alternative is forever.

A well-known phrase is "Butterflies are free". I believe it might come from the movie of the same name, featuring Goldie Hawn, who was just that- free, I always liked the phrase with it's implication of floating and space --

Chapter XVII – Butterflies are Free

The mind can take flight to anywhere. Stomach butterflies give you the courage to overcome – to quiet the nerves –

Be one – mentally, you have the privilege of going and doing – day dream all you want. If the brain doesn't connect with the muscle needed – then work with the one that responds the most –

Butterflies after leaving the cocoon – they go with the wind, the wheelchair slows you down – your mind and desire has no boundaries.

Sing and someone will hear your song.
Moses Bilsky

Been there – Done that
There but for his Grace!

PART TWO OR THE SECOND PART OF THE LONG HAUL BACK

Chapter I– And All The While I Wondered

It's almost three years since I went down the road of physical destruction – fortunately, it was lined on each side and turn with a maturing and patient mind, a loving family, and the financial strength to continue on an almost, and I repeat, almost normal existence. That's not to say, the real battle had been won – actually it was just the beginning.
So what – I have just celebrated my 83RD birthday and I still can't walk. Do I call it being handicapped, or am I crippled? I promise you this - I am not going to accept the former nor will I settle for the latter.

So I have again returned to the R.I.C., And under the watchful eyes and guidance of two great therapists, (Suzanne & Gwen) I am working harder than ever towards new goals. One is to walk somewhere – Anywhere – with a walker. Not one of the numerous dog walkers walking up and down Chicago Avenue with two and three leashes full of wagging tails – but a small three-fold support on which to shuffle the bones and limber the muscles. For a start in that direction, I slowly shuffled 175 ft. today, my occupational therapist right behind dragging a chair should it be necessary to stop and sit, catch my breath, and hear congratulatory remarks from those around me. This moment in my life was most pleasing – but let me finish this later on, and tell you how I got this far after I stopped Rehab in '05.

Chapter II – Why Wait – It's My Weight

One of the worst things that happens when confined to a wheelchair is the inevitable weight challenge. They say the lighter you are the easier it is to shift and manipulate the body to positions of comfort.

So the goal of the handicapped is to lose weight and exercise, in bed, in the chair, in therapy, trying to walk, etc., etc., etc.

So what we really want is lift off. Lift-off – not to the moon, but lift off, out of the wheelchair to wherever.

But I run into a mental blockage when it comes to unreachable goals. It's the mental occupation of thinking about eating. Usually I plan breakfast tomorrow – at lunch today.

My day is usually too busy to think diet control. My daily schedule doesn't allow a moment of free time to think about the betterment of ---- me.

Six Feet Tall, Three Feet Short

A typical busy daily schedule goes something like this:

1. Doing deskwork after breakfast takes three hours right up to my naptime;
2. Then comes wash up, shave time and dress time;
3. Out to street chores or therapy;
4. Back home for naptime;
5. Small cocktail refreshment to brighten the day;
6. At home or out for dinner;
7. Back home;
8. Clean up for bed;
9. Turn on T.V. for nightly news;
10. And just before falling asleep think about breakfast;
11. Wake back up in time to enjoy a midnight nibble;
12. Back to bed – if okay – stay there;
13. If not – up again to bathroom;
14. Then to the kitchen – turn on T.V. and while there, a small snack.

So you see, I always end up back at square one – and therefore – I have no time, free for myself, to be able to think about dieting. Maybe tomorrow I will have a stronger mind set – we'll try – at least we'll see, while I'm having breakfast – and wondering what's for lunch and dinner.

Chapter III – Today Is Today

Call me when tomorrow comes, but until then let me enjoy and fathom the day. I'm really too busy wheeling and buzzing around to think to far ahead – except when it comes to planning breakfast – that, I always have time for – M'M, M'M, GOOD.

My electric cart is referred to by others, as a Harley or Rolls Royce. I bought it with the proceeds of selling my '98 Lincoln Mark VIII. It's mine, paid and driven by me only.

And once you get out on the street, one realizes that life and the world goes on – With or without your participation. Your understanding of friendship makes a tremendous turn around I won't discuss those who don't fit the bill, but let me tell you about somebody I met at Rehab.

By the way- Out patient Rehab is where you actually witness miracles in the making.

This new friend, a licensed attorney, struck down by a Cerebral Hemorrhage 25 years ago, is a real class act. He carries a card explaining his disability - he understands everything, but has trouble forming words in response. If you think the body is complicated, the brain with its connections to commands to allow life it's self. - WOW – What a genius is the designer.

So this gentleman is fun to meet – chat with – figure out his response – see him laugh, manipulate his movements, and meet him on the street corners, totally unafraid to face the unexpected, and witness his confidence in life. I have unlimited admiration of this new friendship, and my wife and I are proud to call him "Friend".

Going back to rehab after almost a year of laziness is like starting all over. It's kindergarten all over again. Getting a prescription from my primary Doctor is easy. He never listened to my reasons for not exercising, had no sympathy for my excuses of being busy and wrote a note to my stroke Doctor saying "Must concentrate on walking". And as he handed it to me, he easily walked out of the examining room.

An appointment to see the Rehab guru took five weeks. I wasn't in a hurry, but indicated I was.

So being examined this time, showed I had leg muscle strength – they were still all there, but not at my command. My job was to wake them up.

"Good Morning Muscles, nice to still have you around. Instead of just being there, how about trying to hold me up for a change. And if you can do that I'll tell you which direction I'd like to travel. From point A to that chair over there for a start. 10 feet – we'll call it point B."

You'd be surprised how things work in the outpatient workout area. Huge room – your therapist with performance folder in hand is immediately in control, and quickly evaluates your needs blending in with her instructions.

First off, it was evident that my two 4-prong canes – left and right handed, were allowing me to be unsteady. We're going to "walk the walk with a different walker". We picked a new one up from the inventory room – filled the papers for Medicare, and stood up unaided so the height could be adjusted. Suddenly, I was back to 6' tall.

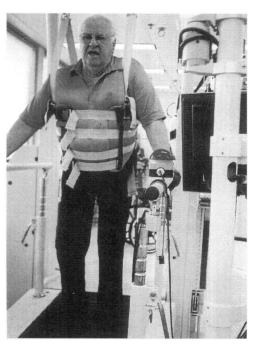

"Learning to walk"

Moses Bilsky

We looked around from where we stood and picked a target about 20'. Made it, but was so glad to sit in the chair behind me. "Catch your breath – that was great." I was told. Now back to the work area.

This large but friendly place had most everything one needs to work dormant muscles. All patients are working to help their weakest extremities. If they are near me, I try to say "Bravo", and they smile.

One of the patients, young, one-leg false, with the face of a determined athlete, hustled with very little teetering to the end of the room and back. I cheered, let go of my walker, clapped and gave him a standing ovation. Why not – I was already standing – my full six feet – and he appreciated the accolade.

Chapter IV – Chicago Is - - - -

This is one big, wonderful, exciting, beautiful, compassionate city. There probably are at least 50 other adjectives to describe each corner and street. But since I'm not always sure how to spell them all, the few above will have to suffice. I still remember how to spell cold, hot, loving, growing and spreading.

I also know that underneath a 4-season spread, slightly hardened, lies a soft considerate city – but finding the suitable program to fit one's needs takes considerable doing.

For me, there is a taxi program. It took me several months to find it. A lot of patience to reach the principle office responsible, and get an appointment to be tested, interviewed and examined. It was and is worthwhile. Chicago Taxi Access Program – economical – you bet- A $1.75 for $13.75 distance on the meter. Don't miss it, it's there to be used and enjoyed.

Another interesting happening, especially on the weekends are the meandering crowds on Michigan Avenue.

Have you ever tried to move through a stationary crowd – sitting down? I have, and do. You've heard the expression, "Everybody marches – nobody watches." Not so when the "Bucket drummers" perform. Then it's everybody stops and listens. It's like a free give-a-way day at McDonalds – by the way, try the Asian Salad if that's part of the give-a-way. It's excellent.

Chapter V – Why So Picky?

Have you noticed there is no time referenced in my story – only an approximation of when and an age relationship? It's not important for the reader to know timing. It's only for me to know, in order to remember the experience and tell a story.

My memory doesn't run in exact lines of sequences of happenings. Every stroke victim will dream, do, or remembers from a thousand moments in their situations. Can you imagine if we all had one happening at the same moment in our illness – nobody would believe, it has to be "I remember that", or "thanks for telling me." "It wasn't quite like that but thanks for letting me know". "I'll watch out and be aware – and not afraid," It's the real purpose of putting my memory to words and paper.

It's kind of like the bible – anybody's bible. Sooner or later you read something and it may have an effect on one's actions. And if it doesn't that's ok too – the words, thoughts, and message remain constant. That's good enough. It's there if you want it.

Six Feet Tall, Three Feet Short

Chapter VI – It's What – Not When

Approximately 50 people have read my first notes from the beginning of my stroke through partial recovery. I also have a list of 50 different reactions. Some found printing errors – spelling errors – one comment, inspirational – another just no comment. Everyone wanted a copy – one person offered and did produce an extra 15 copies to give away. One was sent to their sick friend. Up to this moment I have not had a response from the R.I.C. executives for whom I had originally hoped would realize how appreciative I am for the extra special care I received.

I am sure in time, I will learn an important story was understood, and how grateful I am for all that was done.

I hope this story will serve to help and allow understanding for other stroke victims and their families.

Chapter VII – Sex – Shall We Talk?

No way - - - think, ok. Let me just say you are about to read a blank group of 83 pages. One for each of my years. One through thirty- one is history, subject to the non-disclosure rules of single life. Page thirty-one through eighty-three are subject to the marriage rules of confidentiality. But the last three years of the latter as a stroke victim have remembrances as exciting as all of the previous years, including and plus, a wishful thinking of possibilities I never believed actually existed.

We talk no more.

Your thoughts have to be yours only, as mine are to me.

Chapter VIII – Keep In Mind The Following

1. Invest in prune farms – the returns are excellent;
2. Crying is an expression of the factual inner self – not a weakness;
3. The mind is your personal and private transporter;
   You can visit:
   Heaven or Hell
   The Moon or Ocean Depths
   Think Peace
   War
   Anger
   Hatred
   Love
   Opera
   Pop
   Concerts
   Museums
   Flight
   Mountains
   Volcanoes
   Jungles
   And a million other places; Just be sure that you keep hold of the path
back to reality. A wrong turn and you can end up in trouble.

Moses Bilsky

4. Accept graciously – give generously;
5. Pray frequently to give – rather than receive;
6. Share – it's a great way to enjoy;
7. Thank yesterday, enjoy today, and hope for tomorrow;
8. Somebody is taking care of you. How can you help them?
9. Independence is a desired goal – you have to work for it;
10. Do not touch - - - is a "why" necessary?
11. Are you satisfied with "enough" or do you selfishly want more?
12. If tomorrow starts without you, would that be ok with you?
13. Are you satisfied with yesterday? Maybe you have time to better it in the very next moment;
14. Love at least something, more than yourself;
15. Feeling better – pray it continues;
16. Feeling worse – pray it gets better. Help it along with an upbeat attitude;
17. Finally – may the world find lasting peace and to each of you – Good Health, and may the luck of the gods always be at your side.

Thanks for reading my thoughts and wishes.

Titles Of Writings To Follow:

I.   My Greatest Accomplishment – Forthcoming In – '07 – '08 – '09 – '10 if I'm Lucky.
II.   Am I Blind, Or Is It That I Just Can't See?
III.   How To Compensate Yourself – When You're Down And Out And Poor As Hell.
IV.   When Is Too Much Not Enough?
V.   Why Eat Hot-Dogs, When Your Out Of Mustard?
VI.   My Front Lawn Is My Backyard

ONE MORE DAY

Dear Lord,

I'm surprised I have the audacity to ask of you a favor. Usually my prayers are "Thanks for" and "Bless something or someone". Generally, I think in terms of requesting "good health, long life, happiness and prosperity". And I always end up hoping for Peace and Goodwill in our World.

But I want to pinpoint all of my requests and wishes to one prevailing thought. It comes from my very soul and being – Please Lord, Give Me One More Day. As I view this angry world of ours, I would if I could, change it, for the betterment of all.

I wish I could lighten each burden carried, dissipate dreaded illness, become a rest-haven for the handicapped, share wealth, spread love, remove pain from the injured, allow all to hear music, make sure all eyes could see goodness to be found everywhere, know that trust would never be betrayed, and power never exerted to mislead or destroy.

It's your world Lord, and what a great world it is. Just let me have one more day that I can say to my children, I've tried my best on your behalf. Just let me have one more day to tell my wife of 52 years, I love you more than yesterday and yesteryear. Let me have one more day to remember and savor yesterday. I just want one more day to be able to hope for a better tomorrow.

And please Lord, let me have one more day to try harder to be thankful for today.

Your Obedient Servant,

Moses

Moses Bilsky

For M&M eyes only,   **Jan. 07**

I began this letter when the author arose over a month ago. You have kept me so busy; this letter fell to the bottom of the pile. So it is time it was completed as you both complete me.

Tonight, as often, I am up at 3am, it must be hereditary.

My thoughts are rambling as often & some times I jot them down on a piece of scrap paper, usually to be lost in days to come (just the paper, the thought's continue to float in & out of my days). My thought's are of great letters, things I want to say, but never find the right time & place to complete.

I am inspired by your (Dad) excitement of your newfound documentation of thoughts.
You think this is a new found talent, I know it's not!
All my life you've (M&M) been poetic in your thoughts, speech & parenting.

You have brought me so much pleasure & happiness over the last months by allowing me to be "The California Printer". I am so blessed & happy to be a part of your life & contribute to your happiness today. The greatest gift I have ever received, up there with your (M&M) love, acceptance, trust, friendship & parenthood, was the other day when I received a call from you & modern technology allowed me to see it was you calling - I answered "California Printer". You chuckled like you did when I was 4 watching a Tom & Jerry cartoon. Once you stopped you said "you make me so Happy" That was the finest gift I could receive, to make you chuckle & feel happiness from the heart. I tear'd up thinking of your joy & how wonderful it made me feel to hear you so tickled.

Six Feet Tall, Three Feet Short

And when you (Dad) are chucking, I hear Mom in the background start to chuckle too. Which happens to be the most beautiful music I have ever heard. I wish I had a recording/movie of the two of you chuckling over something so funny. It wouldn't matter the subject –

because when that happens, you can hear the love, trust & friendship through your music.

I wish I lived physically closer to you, so I could stop by & visit with you more often. I really miss being with you & spending time with my best friends! Although, if I lived in Chicago, I probably wouldn't have the opportunity to stay with you overnight when I visit from CA. The snuggling & having the late night visits with you as the late night shows begin are the most precious times to me now & I wouldn't trade them for the world!

So unlike the endless words of the poet Moe, my words today are complete, but my endless thoughts & heartfelt love for you are infinite.

All my Love,
Your California Printer,
Jorie

Moses Bilsky

QUESTIONS ON MY MIND AT MIDNIGHT

1. If a tooth is capped, can it wear it in the house?
2. What does a Brown Cow, do now?
3. Does a cavity in your sweet tooth need to be filled?
4. If I have to March into April, May I take June to dinner?
5. Will the Needle in the Haystack sew the button on my lip?
6. What time is it when good Men come to the aid of our country?
7. Is our Country Yours or Mine?
8. How will I get through the winter, if the last Hershey Bar on earth, melts in October?
9. In a Win Win situation, do you win twice in the same event?
10. When you Hang Tough, is Tough dead?
11. How High is Noon?
12. If we don't know how high is Up, do we know how far down is Down?
13. When it's too late, is that before or after late?
14. From where does the wind come up?
15. When the wind dies down, where did it go?
16. If you're half alive, which half is it?
17. When the right moment comes, does it know it?
18. When the temperature is 50, how far behind is 49, and how far ahead is 51?
19. When the Sun peeps through the clouds, is that Voyeurism?
20. When the lights go out, where are they going?
21. When you buy a blind for the window, are you Blind?
22. When you're held up at gunpoint, are you balanced?
23. Is daybreak broken?
24. Why does an itch need a scratch?
25. When you look for an answer, did it actually hide? Where?
26. Why don't they sell light bulbs by the ounce (oz.)?
27. If still waters run deep. Are they still or running?
28. If you fly off the handle, where do you land?
29. Do walking canes really walk?
30. If you're as quiet as a mouse, can a mouse hear you?
31. What time is quiet time?
32. Is a Fire Sale held in a building, dangerous?
33. Why do most people inherit money and I inherit arthritis?

Six Feet Tall, Three Feet Short

IT @ FOUR AM

Is it? Was it? If it was, what was it?
If it is, where is it? Why is it here?
Did I imagine it? I thought I saw it, but I can't remember what it looked
like.
I wonder if it will return? And if so, when?
From where? Why can't I reach it?
I thought I touched it. It went past so quickly.
I guess it was just a fleeting moment in time.
I hope I didn't waste it. If I get a second chance
to have it, I hope I will appreciate it.

Oh well, maybe I can go back to sleep thinking
I will enjoy it tomorrow.

ODE TO WHOMEVER

What makes us act, and think, and be?
The way we do – that we can see,
How short is life, that we can think.
If you won't try, then why should I,
But I know you can, and so can I.
We must do our best, and show all who care
That tomorrow starts for those who dare.
We're really in charge, of truth or lie –
Which allows us dignity, before we die.

Moses Bilsky

DON'T TELL MY DOCTOR

I'm not as smart as some would think,
    I'm really just quite dumb –
'Cause I fixed my high cholesterol,
    With vodka and some rum.

It has a flavor all its' own
    And potent tho it be –
It's really quite delicious,
    And my favorite recipe.

To some I might be crazy,
    And risk a stroke or two,
But down the hatch it seems to go,
    Real good for me – Not you.

So I have the sweetest pleasure,
    Of drinking just so much,
That I always know the signal,
    Of when I've had enough.

When the wheelchair hits the rug or wall,
    And the sound goes through the house,
I know it's time to head for bed
    And be as quite as a mouse.

And once my head lays on the pillow –
    And a tiny prayer is said,
I finally fall asleep and know –
    I'm safe again in bed.

Six Feet Tall, Three Feet Short

A TEAR BECAUSE

I shed a tear this morning,
    And I'm really not sure why.
It might have been sleep –
    Or dust in my eye.
I just wasn't able to cry.

I asked myself "What's up old Man?"
    Though I didn't expect a reply.
But wondered if life in a wheelchair,
    Was just a slow way to die?
It couldn't be that I was ready –
    With a perfect Wife, and 3 grown kids.
I'd just have to make up my mind to the fact,
    That a self-serving act, is on track, to get back.

To a great life with purpose,
    A busy schedule to complete.
Phone calls, and writings, and fresh air to breath.
    Piano to practice, and life to tease –
That I am here to stay.

That I'm here to stay, until I really leave.
    And skip tomorrow,
From whose time I heavily borrow.

Just think, my cholesterol is only 157.

Moses Bilsky

I KNOW WE CAN

I started out with good intent,
    To write a happy thought
I was so sure that along the way
    The day had been for naught
Why can't the silent mind take time
    For Peace and Love as taught.
By those who know a wish or two
    And a falling star be caught.

Old eyes with tears abound,
    See woman nurse the future.
And raise a child in an austere world
    With perhaps
A little hope for life –
    Not crying eyes with loneliness filled
And chariots heaped with despair
    Galloping steeds trampling war and death
The smell of hope and taste of life
    Why breathe the cold clear air
That stiffens hearts and mind
    When goodness, somewhere, sometime,
Will tend to teach mankind.

When do we stop, and begin to think
    Of you who passed me by,
And didn't care what happened –
    To you, or me, - or why.

Are we just so warped and selfish
    That the time has finely come
To pass an opportunity –
    Or just be done.
No helping hand, nor glance, nor smile,
    To those on the corner alone
In complete despair, with no where to go
    And mumbling thanks – for what?

Six Feet Tall, Three Feet Short

Why – why – why, I cried,
 Can't someone come along
To help with outstretched hand and say,
 I'm here – can I really help?
I don't have much, and I can't stay long,
 But for you I'll take the time,
And do a little thing, or offer hope and thought,
 That can better you in some small way
For care, or word, or perhaps a smile,
 Which now, cannot be bought.

We breathe the same air,
Walk the same land,
Swim in equal waters.
 But some of us choke,
 And some of us stumble,
 And some of us drown.

Help me – help you – help those who need
 From milk and honey – to potato soup.
A hand up the ladder might just be enough,
 To get over a rough spot, on a road too tough
So to those for whom love of God can say –
 The best road is straight and true,
Though dangerous curves
 Lie every where.
I'll try and help you through.

Moses Bilsky

HOLD ON – CUSTER!

When I was a boy of 12 or 10
    And didn't know what's best
I longed for a horse and saddle
    To be able to ride straight west.

So thru the dust, and hillsides green
    I'd wander town to town,
Perhaps to find excitement,
    Or maybe settle down.

I didn't know the need to be
    As cautious as they warned,
But hostile Red's, behind the rocks
    Had gathered in a swarm.

A bugles distant cry I heard
    And to the sound I rode,
T'was Custer leading - sabers drawn
    Yet to bear a heavy load.

I couldn't hide, and couldn't run
    And tight I held the reins,
So I joined the charge and took the lead
    And saw Custer in deep pain.

We closed the circle, stood our ground
    And waited with baited breath
As down they came, and cut us up
    We fought and faced our death.

For some unknown reason
    I looked down upon the scene
And saw me standing there alone
    The fight was over, with blood
On green.

Six Feet Tall, Three Feet Short

So there I was, unscathed thank God,
 And wondered how I escaped –
To be able to remember all this and more
 And keep my memories tape
A moment in the history books
 And the half page it took.

CUT IT FAIR

When is enough – enough,
 And when is too much – too much.
When do I take the lot which is mine,
 And share it some of the time?

Some for me – and some for you,
 And a little for the other guy.
It's not a lot, but it might be right,
 If we shared a piece of the pie.

If we cut it straight –
 And share it even,
And all can taste the sweet.
 The used to be rich, and all the poor,
Get a better chance –
 To be back on their feet.

And start anew –
 And try again,
And politics be dammed.
 I vote for sharing, and lots of caring,
As was originally planned.

Moses Bilsky

I'VE GOT THE WORLD

It ain't easy Magee,
    To try and be me –
When I was one and thirty,
    I walked down the aisle
To a beautiful Lass
    And Knew for sure,
I had the world by the Ass.

But now at home,
    And I lock the wheels,
I nervously can stand –
    To reach for some high object
That my current need demands.
    I go from here to there,
Sitting in my chair
    And thank God for all my blessings.

But my movements are kind of hurting,
    And I'm moving very slow
The wheels in front,
    Often bumps
At times it's unexpected,
    Cause most of holes and cracks
Are truly undetected.

I'm often late –
Please wait –

I'm sitting in the chair.

I push the wheels
    And roll around –
My feet don't touch the ground,
    I try my best to be normal,
And get where I want to go.

So - And –

Six Feet Tall, Three Feet Short

I though when I got married,
    How lucky I should be,
If I was allowed to live with her
    At least to age 83.

I WILL IF YOU WILL

Why are you so superior, and I but
    Mediocre – from your viewpoint?
Yet the way I view it, it is I –
    The superior one,
And you are destined to mediocrity

Does that make sense,
    I don't think so.
How about we reach common ground,
    And admire the qualities of each other.

I used to think that if I only had
    A second chance –And
Maybe you thought perhaps you could do better.

How about putting our love for life,
    And our talents to succeed –
In each others direction,
    Where really lies the need.

And nurture friendship and brotherhood
    And each other's religious preference
So that tomorrow we honor
    Each other's true intelligence.

Moses Bilsky

MY LOVE

I met a woman years ago –
    The most powerful aid of my life.
Who after a short romance,
    Agreed to be my Wife.

I'm not going to bore you with details
    From wedding night 'til now
But we plodded through all the ups and downs
    And got through each one somehow.

And when I loose my courage
    Have questions about my life.
Again steps, to the forefront
    Once more is my wife.

Her strength is always present,
    There's love deep in her eyes
And when I get discouraged
    And can't see where I am
She's there – right near my chair
    And asks – why cry?

A stroke obliterated all my hopes
    And placed me in her care,
Argue or feel sorry for me –
    I wouldn't even dare.
She cleans and works
    And straightens books,
Silver and glass as well.
    The laundry, the iron,
Painting nicks the wheelchair makes.
    Helping me wash, shower
Toilet and things
    Groceries, shopping, meals to fix,
Keeping me happy – all in the mix.
    When my attitude lessons

Six Feet Tall, Three Feet Short

And I want to give up
    I'm shown bluntly how full is my cup.
If a drain's clogged, or something leaks
    All's repaired now, not next week.

No thought of obstacle, no mountain too high
    She does it all, or at least will try.
My God I'm lucky, I'm still alive.
    And I benefit every minute from her
Love and Care
    As I sit in my wheelchair,
And thank God I'm still here.

Moses Bilsky

SECOND CHANCE?

I wonder how?
  And wonder why?
And then I wonder more.
  That we don't look back at history –
And study days of yore.

Have we ever won a war before –
  That we sacrificed a thought.
That equal principle, and men,
  And life could not be bought.

We build and then start over,
  And redesign the world.
Then tumble back,
  And Hope and Pray,
It's our Flag that's unfurled.

Perhaps for us it's right, we think,
  That our way is the best.
But maybe so is theirs you know –
  So let's put it to the test.

Have we tried to change our habit,
  Is it culture that's at stake.
Do we understand our enemies?
  Before it's much too late.

Try Harder – Start Now!

Six Feet Tall, Three Feet Short

ONCE IN FAR OFF MEMORY

Once in far off memory,
    A hope and a dream came true.
We wished for a child of love, and hope,
    So God complied with you.

It didn't matter Boy or Girl,
    Just one – a part of us.
That unified: was sterilized,
    And played and cried and fussed.

How lucky could we three be,
    That later on – one more.
An extra one to love and care,
    So now we totaled four.

We always new they're happy,
    Cause Grand ones bought the toy.
So we rewarded each and all,
    With an extra one – a Boy.

And as we melded all of us,
    Mischief Manor had a mouse.
A pair of M's, and three little J's,
    Allowed us to call – Full House.

Moses Bilsky

A WORD FOR "WELL"

Words that are elegant,
 Or the size of an elephant –
Are often thrown around.
 But if not spelled with love,
Then in those of above
 Sincerity, is never found.

You don't have to be a scholar,
 To earn a true dollar –
And respect from your fellow man
 Just try and be fair,
And learn to share
 And follow God's Great Plan.

That all men are equal,
 Without name or color
And language no barrier too.
 Just don't forget women,
Who are half of the Other,
 Are the only ones you can call Mother.

So all are part of the formula,
 And the mix is quite normal as well.
A little of this –
 And a little of that,
And (What, your expecting a word to rhyme with "well")

Six Feet Tall, Three Feet Short

THE BLACK KNIGHT

Who stands for this fair maiden,
  Whose head lays on the block
That knighthood seems –
  To quick too fade
For a Kingdom soon to block.

And as the ax begins to fall,
  On beauteous neck laid bare.
Her cries are heard from one afar,
  The close ones do not care.

I'll save you soon fair Maiden,
  As soon as I get back.
If all that's left of you,
  Is a bloody head in the sack.

I'll cradle you in my saddle,
  You won't take up much room.
Especially how I'll carry it,
  On a stick at the end of a broom.

Now some might think I'm selfish,
  And no brave-heart at all.
But I know how to save my life,
  And not the ax to fall.

I say yes, and fight for those,
  Who wear the Royal Crown.
And don't have time to do nothing else,
  And never caught lying down.

Pay me well in secret,
  And fatten up the till.
I'll brush it all aside & say,
  I guess it was just God's will.

Moses Bilsky

RHYTHMS

I wish I were a carving knife,
    As sharp as sharp can be.
And cut out human suffrage,
    Like cutting down a tree.

And 'though the forest would lack but one,
    It leaves a space for new to grow.
And sprout a healthier kindness,
    From seeds you try to sew.

From the rhythm of my very soul,
    To all who hear my song.
A new idea with a helping hand,
    Will surely come along.

I write to ask of those who read,
    My each and every word.
Let those who want to try and help,
    Their song – should now be heard.

Six Feet Tall, Three Feet Short

ANOTHER WOMAN

By chance – and not too often
 An opportunity comes along.
When you find a friend of value,
 Who understands your song.

To the best of my recollection
 Our paths only crossed four times.
Several restaurants during when, I don't remember,
 And once again last September.

The last time she was with her daughter,
 As our guest with pleasure.
A visit of importance
 And we could measure
The true joy of friendship.

It wasn't in secret
 But we didn't brag.
And didn't want hurt feelings,
 Or let the cat out of the bag.

And then we used the telephone,
 For laughter back and forth.
And we could talk and have a chat,
 About everything from this to that.
Expressing approval or pleasure –
 Over each written measure.

How lucky I am to have found her,
 With my wife's approval too.
That we have days for each to enjoy
 For me, and us, and you.

53

Moses Bilsky

HOME

I move around the house at night –
    The wheelchair makes no sound.
And poke a little here and there.
    It's easy without a crowd.

My wife has moved the furniture,
    And made a passage thru –
To the other side of where I was
    To find that "nothings new"

The phrase of "been there – done that"
    Seems to ring a bell
And being somewhat mobile
    Is better than being in hell.

There was a time, when I lay in bed
    And couldn't even turn over.
So that everything had to be done for me,
    I was not in a bed of clover.

With my mind made up
    And quite determined
I followed my therapist lead
    And doing as told
It began to unfold
    I can do it. – I will succeed.
I GOT HOME.

Six Feet Tall, Three Feet Short

MOONLIGHT

What if the moon arose one night,
 And turned the other way?
Would that new phase indicate,
 There's trouble come next day!

We're supposed to be under its' influence –
 With destiny be dammed.
But I believe it isn't so,
 Cause life goes on as planned.

And I control the helm and sail
 And chart my course to be,
So my days and nights aren't controlled
 By phase one, or two, or three.

I don't believe God laid a plan
 That allowed us little choice.
So instilled in us was consciousness,
 To be expressed by our small voice.

Speak up all you citizens, for this country that is ours
 Balance truth and love – shout from towers
To rebound through hill and dale,
 So the moon turns back, and orange to pale.

And smiles for all to see –
 "Especially Me"

Moses Bilsky

THE LAST DANCE

Early in our togetherness, and engrossed in raising a family, and earning a living, we, like many loving couples, relied on home entertainment – so we took up dancing. Six couples and one pro teacher - and each other's home once a week.

Push the furniture; plan cocktails and light refreshments, along with cocktails – after an hour workout. We were all fast learners. We stumbled, laughed, bumped scratch the floors, but learned a new step every week. Warned by the instructor 'don't go public yet" sounded stupid. What's so hard about memorizing, on-two, one-two-three? Got it.

We're ready. Dinner date at the "Buttery" room, in the Ambassador West. The place to be seen. Music perfect. One cocktail, and while waiting for food service – on the floor we go. I'll lead. Let's see – which foot is on ONE. Can't get started. I touched the shoulder of an elder gentleman, and asked "get us started (the teacher was right, "Don't go public yet.")

Patience prevailed, and following our new instructor – we were "one – two – one – two – threeing" with the best of them.

So for almost 50 years, here and there, we moved to the music of the night. December 30, 2003 was exciting. We chose to celebrate New Years Eve the night before – skip the private club at extra high pricing, and take in the scene at the Drake Hotel's Palm Court.

My wife was beautiful. Gowned to perfection – the envy of many, and I felt the part of a proud Peacock. On the dance – floor – a great trio. My arm

Six Feet Tall, Three Feet Short

around a tiny 21" waist – when I turned her around it never let go – and sensually slid 360 degrees – thrilled –you bet.

And then fate stepped in – March 30, 2004 I became a stroke victim. Have never been able to hold again, as I remember that special night.

Several times we went back to just hear the music, but it was never the same.

There was never again the egotistical thrill of a proud entrance, to show a stunning wife off – I loved the envious looks bestowed, as they watched my lady glide to our table.

In a wheelchair – call security at the front door – to a back elevator, a third level - down a long hall, to a second elevator which stopped in some passage way – to a ramp, with two hotel people pushing and balancing the wheelchair by four feet to another hall. There my wife had to push me to the Palm Court. Through tables and past sofas to our reserved spot. And the music didn't start – they changed it to and hour later. It was our last visit.

Now for 52 years we learn what LOVE is. Its "been there, done that – TOGETHER". We've found that the true meaning of our marriage vows "In sickness or in health", "richer or poorer" be sure and underline Together; underline Sickness, under line Poorer.

Now you know how to spell LOVE. It's all of the above. And it occurred in OUR world. Underline Our, capitalize OUR – put "our" in quotation marks. And put OUR in giant letters. And with all of the above – you're just coming close to understanding "LOVE".

How I would LOVE to be able to hold my wife like I used to - on the dance floor - or any floor – if I could only stand with out aid. It's so little to ask for - so I pray, "Just one more dance."

Moses Bilsky

SOUL KEEPER

It stays with me from morn' till night,
    And registers my presence.
Yet cares not who or what I am –
    As long as I have essence.
I think my thoughts original,
    Tho deep within me sits
My history –
    Has been stamped.
And framed a true impression
    From whence I came
And might yet wander.

In between, I mold a path
    Which follow, I must do.
Up and down – in and out,
    And to myself be true.
The family tree was rooted
    When life developed man
And down the stream of rock and cranny
    Slowly – my life began.

History, religion and culture –
    All play a determining part,
Of what was – and is – and will be
    Including music, prayer and art.
Strengthen my arm, increase my stride
    And educate my mind.
To give me time for happenstance,
    And offer another the chance –
To be- just to be –
    No more – no less.
Exact and pure, with little doubt.
    My soul to cry out –
I'm here – I am – I am.

Six Feet Tall, Three Feet Short

LIFE IS A PILL

There are pills that heal – and those that kill,
    And many are in between.
All shapes and sizes, large and small
    And some – never take at all.

The little ones, from fingers slip –
    The large ones catch in my throat.
And some are so important,
    That I write myself a note.

If I miss the one for A.M.
    And the second one at night –
I have to wait till round the clock,
    When timings just right.

Blood pressure, nerve pain, and thinners
    Are early morning tastes.
I'm also watching, swelling, diuretics
    And channel blocking,
Along with certain types of waste.

Perhaps I worry to being over-exposed,
    And ask my Doctor what for?
His answer is plain and simple –
    "So you can reach age 84".

Moses Bilsky

THINKING TO WRITE ABOUT

Dreamer
    I can't believe I write as I do,
And think in dreams going by.
    So I hurry and jot them down at once –
Hoping they don't make me cry.

Quote: You cannot anticipate appreciation –
    Only express it after the fact, or in retrospect.

Songs of my Father – he loved to tell, and he loved to laugh.
"A horse and a flea, and three blind mice,
    Sat at the corner shaking dice.
The horsey slipped, and fell on the flea –
    And the flea said, that's a horse on me."
                OR
"A fly flew in the grocery store –
    He flew right in the open door.
He lit on the sugar and he lit on the ham –
    And he wiped his feet on the grocery man."

I would laugh – and he would laugh –
    And there was admiration in our eyes.

New book title:
    "From a stroke of Inspiration."

New book title:
    "Mind my stroke – This is what I think!"

Today's Question:
    Who Sir, are you Sir?
    If your not my keeper –
    Then who are you Sir?

Truism:
Do not pass up the moment of valued extended friendship. It may not be
offered again.

Six Feet Tall, Three Feet Short

Just thinking:
Today I saw the sun. The same sun I have seen for eighty-three years. The older I get – the more beautiful it becomes. It's not a fixation, but it certainly is warming. How beautiful, even when in the middle of winter.

I DUN IT FORBIDDEN FRUIT!

Yep, I da one dat dun it. Don't know why –
Just felt like it. Didn't plan it, jus went ahead an' don it.

Felt good too – 'twas my free right – so I done it. It ain't agin' the law – an even if it twere – I wasn't seen doin it.

And I done it with my best girl. We popped the pop – shot the shot. We done tracked the trick – tricked the truck – trucked down to 87th street in winnet – lit the light – fired the fire and warmed da heart – mine – hers – and ours.

Yesterday twas too early – tomorrow too late. The time hit us like a hammer – lust and hunger set in, and we wasn't going to wait any longer. We reached out and grabbed – our fingers, tense with anxiety slipped through, past around, and into the warm substance. It was sticky – our hands shook with excitement – we felt for the one we thought would satisfy – there – got it. Damn that popcorn's good.

Moses Bilsky

FULL – HALF - EMPTY

There are always people who love you,
    And make every effort to say –
It's not always been perfect,
    But please – hang on and stay.

Just a little while longer
    I know you can if you try.
And again I say – if you can,
    Then certainly, so can I.

There's always a tomorrow,
    And I'd really like to see,
Your smile shine through my teary eyes,
    While you are holding me.
And many times I ask myself,
    Is this the last sip from my cup?

That famous cup of life –
    With a hand we lightly grab,
Always asking – full – half or empty?
    Of life, and joy, and love
Or leaking to half – so we sip more slowly
    Hoping we can still laugh.
At those who think they know
    When the cup will ultimately smash.

That a warm embrace, through which we trace
    Our legacy with pride and plan –
From the very moment
    Our marriage began.

Six Feet Tall, Three Feet Short

LUCK

What is it with Life?
 That we try so hard to stay.
Yet days sometimes are many
 And we want to go away.

To a place of quite solitude –
 That knows not anguish or pain,
Where the body can rest finally,
 To life's melodious refrain.

But we're built with fight and stamina
 And a heart that wont give up
So we surround our selves with special love,
 Finding courage from above.

Talk about Luck!

CARDS

If today is not exciting
And tomorrow is full of blah!
Does that indicate we're stupid
And don't deserve the draw.

Of Ace's high –
Or Jack's to open –
Or perhaps a Royal Flush?

Is life just a boring card game?
And we no longer feel the rush –
Of the unexpected –
Or yet to be detected –

The card that fate deals us.

Moses Bilsky

WHY?

Today is not a happy day –
    Tho I really don't know why.
Perhaps I'm not so grateful
    For blessings – nor do I always try
But regardless of trying
    I end up crying – from aches and pains.
And pray I have the courage –
    To not think of dying
And trying – be not in vain.

No one suffers alone –
    When those you love stand by
They feel the trial and effort
    It takes for me to try.

Tho pills and advice are needed,
    For the comfort they provide.
They don't correct the problem
    Just allow it all to slide –
Into hours, and days
    with little relief –
And test the metal of mindless thought
    To question –
    Is it all for naught?

Why are we here?
Why do we fight?
    Thru long days –
    And endless nights.

So I wake up crying,
Tho I'm not afraid of dying –
I'm just tired of trying.

Six Feet Tall, Three Feet Short

STRUT ON

I'm not sure, if I believe
    That what I write is true
But it doesn't matter what I believe
    As long as you believe it too.

I look at life from a mountain top –
    And question the highs and lows
Can I climb higher - or slip and fall
    And no longer take life's blows.

Pick me up – talk to me square,
    I need just one more chance,
To explain to those who love me,
    We still have time to dance
And hold, and squeeze, and pray tonight,
    So tomorrow we can prance.

And I mean strut baby – just strut.

Moses Bilsky

WHAT YOU DON'T SEE – IS WHAT YOU GET

Early last year and in jest – I thought I would title a writing "My front lawn, is my backyard". I refer to so many instances, of not being completely honest, or nakedness. Rather, so much of life is described as syrup – and damn little pancakes or waffle to be discovered.

It's ok to have a front – but not a cover-up. There should be a path to the backyard, where honesty, image, and worth, are the true core of who we are.

We normally all plant flowers and pretty bushes in the front – the weeds in the back allowed to spread. The basement was great, but behind the furnace, we stack the broken screens. We wash the car on weekends, especially if going out with friends.

Life plays constant tricks. Fool'em – pass'em – juggle'em – stack'em. Why? Because we look better. Clean shirts – fancy dress – jewelry to show in evenings – jeans to push the grocery cart – haircuts for Holidays – beauty shop for weekends. Tip for Hotels – when was the last tip given to a newsboy or drugstore employee? Tip your cap to a police officer – scorn the traffic woman.

The Opera calls for special seats – Church and Synagogue, get there early.

My Mother was special although – she was "ALL FRONT LAWN" from morning 'till night. Even a meal in the kitchen, or for a sandwich, called for silver and serviettes.

Let your front door be as warm and friendly as the back porch with the grill and stacked firewood. May your refrigerator be as tasty as the day before grocering – your bar have a few extra tastes besides your own preference, and your purse-strings be loose enough for a hungry face in the crowd.

Believe me – you don't need to love the world – just your fellow man.

In all of ONE moment – your backyard will be identical to your front lawn.

Six Feet Tall, Three Feet Short

GOOD BYE WITH LOVE

What courage and strength it takes,
　　To step aside and watch –
And hold your breath, with fingers crossed
　　Being helpless –
As the mind thinks back – like hop-scotch.

And reflections, which once were fun,
　　Flash in and out of reality.
Leaving one standing, with perhaps a tear,
　　To wonder of Life's triviality.

There's not much one can do,
　　But know within themselves –
That always "Their Best" was there.
　　For each and all to delve.

So we wait, and pray in a corner
　　Of one's mind, so not to be seen –
That the passing of a loved one,
　　Affects all that have ever been.
As son, daughter, sister, brother –
　　Friend, neighbor, Rabbi or Priest,
Have a thought in mind at best –
　　For the safety of the one for whom they pray.
To travel on God's Wings, to Peace and Rest.

Moses Bilsky

TIRED? NOT ME.

There are days that I feel sorry,
    For myself, and others as well.
And wonder if the effort is worth it,
    To rise from the pits of hell.

My line of vision is only so high,
    My reach is often short.
My leg is just a drag to drag,
    And certainly gives no support.

I'm always asked, "how do you feel"?
    So I put on a happy show.
And as long as my wife stays near me
    I try to be ready to go.

But the truth of the matter is shocking
    When I can't even reach for a shelf.
I scream and shake in silence,
    And feel sorry for my self.

And all the things that are natural
    For a human being to do.
Or expected of a husband –

And at that moment my wife entered the room –
And I said – "I'm so tired, that I" –
And my comment was cut short with –
"And don't you think I am too"?

This Lady – my wife of 53 years – this caretaker – this Saint, who goes 16 hours a day on my behalf, for my welfare, for our daily needs and necessities, who lends her hands and back to my every need – crosses the street and watches people and traffic for my safety – opens handicapped doors, clears aisles – walks beside me, with a hand on my shoulder to tell me she's there – while I ride – gets me in and out of bathrooms etc. – helps me dress, and performs every function possible to complete my daily life – with whom I share a little "nightcap on the rocks", around 11:00p.m.

Six Feet Tall, Three Feet Short

– adjusts the heat or air-conditioning in the middle of the night for my comfort – changes my sheets at 3:00 a.m. if necessary – and more – and more – and more.

And I have the audacity to say "I'm tired". What am I thinking? How dare the idea even enter my mind.

No way – The phrase and word "Tired", has been expunged from my vocabulary, from my thoughts, or any outward effort. I won't even yawn in the presence of a Saint.

Life leaves you with a thousand questions, but I am sure of one thing – She loves me – and I her.

A BROTHER LOST

I grieve for some unknown reason –
    For something I have lost,
Yet didn't want to keep.
So in my mind while trying to sleep –
    I searched and wondered what the cost?
Of mental anguish – to feel the guilt.
    As the years slipped into a lifetime –
And formed a bond of family ties,
    That lacked love, respect, and trust.
While jealous vibes became the barrier,
    To brother rejecting brother.
The youngest extending friendship –
    In many different ways.
The oldest always wary with warped mentality,
    Rejected many chances,
And died this very day.

How sad, how very sad –
That Peace came after losing.

Moses Bilsky

NO TIME OUT

The water's rolling waves and chop,
 Are now laden with snow and ice.
The shoreline's beaches are hard with crust
 As beach chairs gather dust.

But it won't be long before the sun sets high
 And worshipers gather to play –
Ice cream vendors stroll along,
 Right through the long hot day.

I wonder if tomorrow brings
 The same bright day for all
Or is it the last day of summer –
 And tomorrow, the first day of fall.

Let the little children play,
 In the waters edge of froth,
For life adds years to quick to count –

We're only here for a moment!

NO RESPONSE

I think the time has come –
 That when displeased I hum –
In doing so, I try to say
 I hope the day soon goes away.
I pay no-never-mind to most,
 Of things I cannot change,
And hum at those that wrankle me,
 'Cause "they", just have to be.

No one hears me groan and moan,
 As I wonder why manners are lost?
What is wrong with "thank you" –
 How much do you think that would cost?

Six Feet Tall, Three Feet Short

When you stay at home like I do –
    And wheel around the house,
I take the time to write my thoughts –
    And send for all to enjoy.
Yet only one of forty,
    Bother to respond.

Perhaps I trample privacy.

STILL TIME LEFT

I often think of dying
    I understand there's no pain,
But I'm left with worry on my mind,
    That what is there to gain.

It certainly isn't peace of mind,
    For that too is certainly lost,
And to have to give up on all the good things,
    My gracious – what a cost.

Why should I sacrifice family and friends,
    And perhaps a party or two
When then, all that would be left would be nothing,
    And I wouldn't even have you.

And back beyond horizon unknown
    You'd wonder why I left,
And I wouldn't be there, when you needed me most,
    Was this God's wish or a ghost?

I'm not going – and you can't make me leave,
    I'll fight to the end – with a trick up my sleeve.
We'll still have a scotch together,
    And I know we both will say,
We are lucky – we have another day.

Moses Bilsky

A NECESSARY CUT

Fearing fear is one thing
    Being afraids' another
Having nightmares while awake
    Allows internal shakes.

Tomorrow by a surgeons hand
    I choose to allow him to cut
A growth they say must come out
    From my backside near my butt.

I'm sure I'm safe, with my wife around
    And waiting close, nearby.
But it's the interim of being along,
    That makes me want to cry.

So I can't sleep
    And I'm nervous as hell
But maybe tomorrow
    I'll have a story to tell.

Of how I overcame my fears
    To return home safe and sound
And looking back, and thanking God –
    I'm sure I lost two pounds.

P.S. I changed my mind, in the middle of the night.
    And at 3AM cancelled all.
And slept soundly from 4 to 8 –
    I'll reconsider in the Fall.

Six Feet Tall, Three Feet Short

MIX AND MATCH

Me thinks the minks will play tonight,
    And dance around their pens –
'Cause Mrs. Mink is winking
    And strutting in front of her den.

Albert and Peter, and perhaps even John,
    Are not quiet old enough –
    And don't line up just now.
Since service time for each of them, -
    Is waiting for their chow.

But Sally Mink's been around the block
    And her patience is about to be tried.
Unless she's approached by some old bloke
    And gets to her (or at least tries)
Before he keels over and dies.

Why is it that a minks prefer minks
    And otters prefers otters –
So they don't play with each other
    To become cuffs and collars.

And so it is with life I guess,
    That we each seek out our own.
And strut on down the course of life –
    At least until we're grown.
And finally learn – tho sometimes late
    About the seeds we've sown.
That Salt and Pepper, or sweet and sour
    Go well on any plate.

Moses Bilsky

IMAGINATION

Today – I bought a Whorehouse,
    From back in the corner of my mind.
I thought I would because I could –
    It would service any kind.

I planned it carefully, and laid out rooms
    For excitement and comfort for sure,
Each one with a purpose, of their desire –
    Not necessary to try and put out a fire.

Tho one's nerves might be frayed,
    I would still get paid.
For rent, and heat, and lights if any –
    So I could count my spoils to the penny.

News papers delivered – with no news to read,
    Music all soft tracked.
A place so desirable, and you would see
    That each and everyone would come back.

There'd be no rush in the mornings
    With breakfast served past noon.
While the staff cleaned up
    And straightened every room.

So all would have a pleasure
    For what ever they would wish,
All they need to do –
    Is write it on a list.

Free membership for ninety and over,
    With no exception made.
A contract on the dotted line,
    Assured me of getting paid.

And once, when I could afford it –
    To the city I would move,

Six Feet Tall, Three Feet Short

And lead a most up righteous life.
But I know I'll wake up in the morning,
And lucky me, I'll still be with my wife.
"There is no substitution for the Good Life."

ANYTHING IS POSSIBLE

My fingers hurt
    And my back is stiff,
So when in the wheelchair
    I wonder if –
That years ago, when making plans
    To conquer the World
And train my hands
    For a concert show,
That when the curtain would rise
    And the Steinway set –
Top open – bench back
    Keys polished,
    Shiny whites,
    And thirty – six black,
I'd walk on stage,
    Acknowledge my presence
To Maestro and Baton,
    And sit poised to accomplish,
A life's dream.

Then back to reality my mind would dart,
    On the street of adventure,
In my electric cart.
    Visiting here, and sometimes there –
All would be well.

If I could only breathe fresh air,
    To replenish my spirit,
And hope to be –
    Stymied by nothing,
And totally free.

Moses Bilsky

NEW MOON

I've reached a precarious age today,
    And I'm standing on the edge of tomorrow
So I'm not sure how I will respond
    To the extra time I borrow.

I hope and trust I'll use it well –
    And share it along the way
So anyone can benefit
    And HELP make all O.K.

It's after 3AM right now –
    And I'm writing at my desk.
While gazing out the window
    From which I look due West.

And there it was, in all it's glory
    A yellow – orange moon.
A little on its' backside
    With only half to see,
Still romantic as ever,
    But there's only me –

Yet in my mind's eye,
    I held my wife in grasp.
And hope and prayed
    That all the world
Would learn to LOVE at last.

Six Feet Tall, Three Feet Short

Moses Bilsky

IT'S NOW OR NEVER

In the middle of the night –
    When shadows move,
And the wheelchair slides
    Over cracks and grooves.
There's a certain quiet that creeks-
    From the city below.
Tho the lights are aglow,
    And they twinkle.
Like a Birthday cake
    Lit up for all ages.

So where do the shadows go?
    That remain in my mind.
Which seem to bounce from door knob to wall,
    To ceiling and hall.
Am I in control of who I am?
    Or will I allow life to be just a sham.

What purpose do I serve?
    For God and thee-
Or is every thought designed by me.
    Self serving? Well it better not be.
Because – Because –
    Well it just better not be.

I affect the place where I live,
    And of those around.
My thoughts of the world,
    Must some way abound.
And be heard – the killing must stop.
    Love and compassion begin
And it starts from within –

    Come on – Get with it!

Six Feet Tall, Three Feet Short

FUNNY?

Today I had a request to write a poem,
    That doesn't mention sadness, sickness or death.
    And no more stories of troubles, famine, drought or mess-
But find something to laugh about,
That's contagious – for all ages.

So I dig in my past,
    As deep as I dare
And try to remember good times
    So I minus in tens from eighty-four
And start over at age four
    When all I remember was Mother
And was told I had sister and brother.

But my Father managed a Department Store,
    And visiting him was fun –
'Cause the candy was free'
    And you could hide in the aisles –
With a huge bathroom in which to pee.

So a kid at four –
    Couldn't ask for more,
Unless it was to discover girls
    But that had to wait
Until I was eight –
    When I could write and spell
And you won't know
    How I could raise hell,
And I was only in second grade.

Moses Bilsky

A NEW CHANCE

I wake up to sadness on my mind,
    And troubles in my heart
That somewhere in the world of ours
    The day is not off to a happy start.

I don't know how to help it –
    I just feel the pressure of concern
And wonder if my involvement
    Will help someone else to learn.

I can't tell my own, what course they should take
    Or which problem they should solve,
I only hope and pray each night
    That daylight brings resolve.

But perhaps if I watch and quietly wait
    And pray for solutions unknown,
This troubled old world, will find a way –
    And give each and all
    A chance,
For a brand new day.

WE NEED

There's a fire in my heart,
    And I'm not sure of purpose, - or why.
I do know someone suffers,
    And some even die.

It's all the false promises,
    We unknowingly make,
That creates situations,
    Leaving chaos in their wake.

Six Feet Tall, Three Feet Short

Republicans blame the Democrats
    And they take the opposite stand,
So that pretty soon all are bragging,
    To the tunes of a marching band.

We don't need lawyers
    And certainly not judges,
To further muddle,
    The politicians grudges.

I think what's really needed,
    Are the hard working gals and guys,
Who handle their hardships
    And look straight in your eyes.
To find amicable solutions,
    With as little as possible – pollution.
And fighting and willing to die
    For the true American Constitution.

How noble are those true citizens,
    Who take up the challenge of the day,
And find a way to a hard earned rest,
    And oftentimes
Not enough pay.

This world needs doers –
    Let the braggers step aside,
And each of us receive God's smile,
    And the approval nod it takes
For the extra mile, beneath our feet
    And for the happiness it makes.
For this great country we dearly love
    May we protect our boundaries true.
I will. I hope you will too.

Moses Bilsky

ADVISE

Getting old –
  Is for the bold,
And you learn to hang on tight
  To each and every day,
My friend –
  Hoping you can bend.

To at least put on a shoe, or two
  If someone's helping you.
The first trick you have to master –
  Is getting out of bed,
Do not slip from covers – to chair
  When first you clear your head.
So when you push the wheels to go
  That's a good sign your not dead.

In and out of the bathroom,
  And down the hall you go
To check the fridge, and have some toast,
  With prune juice –
Which helps the most.

And so the day begins on high,
  With schedules to be met,
So that on your list –
  Is carefully placed
What medicines you missed.

Worry not - the drugstore's near
  And off you go by noon.
To poke hear and there a little
  And say hello to anyone
That makes a friendly nod.
  And makes you feel a part of life,
So you can thank God –
  For the privilege of being alive.

Six Feet Tall, Three Feet Short

It may not be all sweet and honey,
    And the pain of life hangs on
But at least you have some fun
    Providing you don't run out of money.

And when you do – I hope you pray
    To find a way
To continue struggling through life
    That's easy for me to say,
I'm lucky – I have a Saint for a wife.

But there truly are ways to compensate
    And you must honestly try –
Cause most of the answers are within you
    Long before you die.

But I'm told to stop writing about sadness,
    That the sun will come out and shine
Upon you and yours –
    And mine and ours
If we have faith and trust
    Like I told you, you must –
Take prune juice first,
    And the day will take care of itself.

Moses Bilsky

A PIPE DREAM

A golden lady, from out of the past –
    Entered my life today.
And fifty – three years of untruth's passed by
    So that a blemished past
    Just faded fast
And happiness set in once more.

The years of missing her –
    Were covered with innuendos and lies,
So my piano shelf stayed empty
    With only a vision of ties,
    To what used to be –
And remained constant in memory and mind.

It stayed that way,
    Until a brother was lost,
    And Son began a new life.
And honored his Grandmother's wishes
    As tho the past were cut with a knife.

So once more the Pipe Dream stood beautiful
    In charge of all she surveyed –
And blended with music and rhythm
    Which only love could convey.

    From my piano –

Six Feet Tall, Three Feet Short

RING THAT BELL

Thank God for good old Alexander – Bell that is.
　　He helps me through the day,
And gets me able to say Hello –
　　And bye the bye – Good Bye.

What a pleasure it is, to hear from a friend –
　　Whether it's news or not.
At least it tells me who or what,
　　Before I think that most forgot.

Of the friendships forged – and good times had,
　　And of thoughts, both good and bad.
So when the phone rings a last –
　　I know I'm not placed in the past.

Please call – at least to say hello.

Moses Bilsky

FUN THOUGHTS

Part I
KITCHEN RULES
1. Do not read using light in oven.
2. Do not turn over partially cooked eggs with a spoon.
3. Matches are not required to turn on electric stove.
4. Never serve Lox on an English Muffin.
5. A hammer is not a kitchen utensil.
6. Allow at least 30 minutes to prepare instant meals.

Part II
JUST THINK
If I had a cow -
 I'd keep it for now,
And forever have milk and cream.
 In the elevator he won't fit
So he'll climb the stair -
 Would anyone care?
If he lives with us.
 And to visit his friends,
We'll take a bus-
 Think of the fun,
While on the run-
 With everyone staring,
And saying -
 What now!
 A brown cow.
However – Being allergic to dairy
 There's no magic fairy
That allows a cow – to live with me now
 I believe it's too soon
Since he already jumped -
 Over the moon.

Six Feet Tall, Three Feet Short

TIME

I'm not sure what it really means,
    Since it's thought of in so many ways.
When you ask "is it time"?
    Does it carry "Now" "or later"
Or is it actually referring to days.

I used to think, "Time was of the essence"
    When making forward plans.
Until I knew life it self,
    Was the quickest of all the scans

Can time stand still?
    Or be counted over again
Will it allow a moment of thoughtfulness?
    And the mind thinks back through life,
So as to rest on a memory of lasting love.
    And know winter snows have spring thaws.
For the joy of life appears constant.

So when asked, "What time is it?"
    Remember the sunrises and sets.
    Season's change, the moon is there,
    And stars above, life breathes –
    The time is now, and love is constant.

Moses Bilsky

DOCTOR

Sometimes life is sweet,
    And sometimes life is short
But for quality that is neat,
    Which you always want to repeat –

Then find the right Doctor.

It doesn't matter the hurt –
    Or location of the pain,
Just be sure that when you need one
    There's nothing to lose –
So consider the gain.

And make a wise choice for a doctor.

Young or old,
    Skinny or bold,
Experience mounts
    And manners count.

Can he analyze, and not surmise

As the years slip by
    With the need increasing
For visits, consultations, and tests,
    Does your doctor heed all –
And answer a night call,
    With a smile in his voice
And suggestions knowledgeable
    For comfort, with wisdom,
To lay aside fear of the unknown.

My Doctor does.

And when you're tired of trying,
    Yet afraid of dying

Six Feet Tall, Three Feet Short

His eyes are of kindness,
        And strength of comfort,
With charitable love
        And caring hands,
Words of wisdom –
        Researched medicines –
Professional follow-ups ,
        All this makes his file
Appear like a reference library.

You bet I have a doctor
An equal does not exist.

Not before – Not now – Not tomorrow.

I hope you're as lucky as me
And find the right doctor for you.

My Doctor –
        What his name you ask?
        I don't remember –

But I do know all his telephone numbers!
        And I'm not telling.

Moses Bilsky

AN OLD POKE

It's okee doke,
    When you're an old poke,
To push the wheels with your feet.
    But if in a race –
With another old poke,
    It's not fair when you cheat.

When one in a chair
    Pass others who care
They smile with a look of pain
    'Cause they know too well
They're come back from Hell
    And they used to walk with a cane.

It's interesting though,
    Since they all seem to know
To give up means to die.
    So pushing on, like the pain is gone
They smile as best as they can.

I'll bet you don't notice,
    As they pass they salute
Which signals we try –
    To go further in life, than just die.

Black or White – Brown or Grey
    They try to go on –
With each day as it comes.
    Regardless of rain or shine
They smile and salute
    And acknowledge the effort
It takes to stay alive.

My God, I admire
    Their spirit and trust
And know that I too must
    Find the strength,

Six Feet Tall, Three Feet Short

To push and conquer my fear,
    And hope I'm able to see
At least to the end of the year.

IN THE RIVER

Good morning Mrs. M'Gillikuty –
    And how are you this bright day?
As you can see, the sun is shining.
    Won't you come out and play?

We'll stroll through town,
    And picnic in the park,
On the lawn so green, by the river
    Flowing almost as high
As last year's water mark

Careful now, you're close to the edge.
    One step and you might slip –
The currents' fast and the waters cold,
    And I can't swim, if you fall in.

So let me ask you one more time
    Do you love me – yes or no?
If yes, I'll try and save you,
    But no, I'd let you go.

Don't hold so tight –
    You'll make me fall –
It's not my fault if I didn't call
    I told you I was busy.

Her name was Sara Jane Kominski,
    And it was just a one-night stand.
Help me – grab my hand – I can't hold on
    Please Mrs. M'Gill….. and no one heard me.

Scream!!!

Moses Bilsky

WHAT IF

If I had a penny
    For any thought
    If I had any
I'd be rich -
    If time didn't run out.

If I had a nickel
    For each time I'm in a pickle
I'd be rich -
    If time didn't run out.

If I had a dime
    For every time
I thought about money
    I'd be in clover and honey.

If I had a quarter
    For each time I bet -
Would I finally get,
    A chance at winning.

If I had a dollar
    Would I give a holler
That it was all mine -
    To keep!

What if I won the Lotto?
    Would it make a difference?
If I shared - or not
    Can friendship be bought?

Is tomorrow - another day?
    With one more chance to pray!

Six Feet Tall, Three Feet Short

A VIEW FROM A SEAT BETWEEN WHEELS

Dreamers who dream,
    And hope dreams come true –
Differ from doers who dream,
    And make dreams come true.
So that doers who do
    Make it happen –
And so could you, if you dream too.

But lets digress for a moment – what do I really dream – what's my immediate dream – just wanting to wake up. First I try to find a position of comfort, I stretch out flat on my back and unintentionally think of Jesus Christ. At least he arose – so I will at least arise "out of bed".

So now I have foolish fun thoughts. My wife is my best audience – so while she is making my bed, I tell her of my busy plans, and how important I am. My favorite places in the house are – the toilet, the refrigerator, and the bar – the latter only at 5:00PM.

Then I write. When finished, I call and read to my editor, my brain ramblings. If she approves – I fax to my California Printer – back to me and on to my Chicago Production Company. Then there is distribution planning, to building residents of my choice, and mailings to my friends.

So you see, my day is filled with excitement like –
Breathing, getting dressed, eventually getting outside for a little airing
And then back to the toilet etc., etc., etc.,
And it starts all over again.

Now back to dream status. As long as I see the day – and get through it with My wife – that's a dream come true.

Moses Bilsky

A PURPOSE FOR AN ACTIVE MIND

Several days ago, I received in the mail, a chance to finally be rich. An offer from Commerce Clearing House said if I did this and that, and perhaps chose one magazine from approximately 3000 listed, I would be greeted at my door with lights, cameras, TV announcers and a 3 X 6 foot check for $10,000,000.00

Why not - I could use the extra money for doctors, nurses, tests and pills. The completed entry went in the mail this morning. I was so proud I had found the courage to even consider my action.

So feeling convinced I know I will win, my wife and I went out for our daily chores.

Upon our return, in our mail was a blue windowed envelope addressed to me only – not Mr. and Mrs. It said URGENT. So after the quickest bathroom stop I have ever made, I went right to my desk and opened the urgent letter.

It said it's possible, I was a winner of $2,000,000.00
if I called the indicated 800-telephone number. I immediately dialed.

The Conversation went like this –

"Your name please?"
    Moses Bilsky
"Mr. Bilsky, may I have your Zip code?"
    60611
"If you can find your special code number – May I" –
    Without hesitation I rattle it off.
"You will be a guest of George Hamilton, here in Florida"
    Great, I really like him.
"What would you do with so much money?"
    Leave it to my children.
"We will fly you to Florida"
    I only fly 1st class.

Six Feet Tall, Three Feet Short

I'm in a wheel chair, so I need to have my caretaker with me.
"That's perfectly all right"
I would have to include two extra people as they have to lift me up and about.
"I'm sure we can handle that problem also.

"Would you want $70,000 each year for 30 years, or would you want to accept $1,000,000 only?"
I'll take the million now please.
"May I ask why you prefer the smaller amount?"
We'll you see – I'll be 84 in September and I'm not sure if I'll be around for the full 30 years. I think receiving less will be better for me right now.

"I think your probably right. Is your telephone
312-654-5789
Yes M'am.
"And I have your Zip code?"
Yes M'am.
"I know Mr. Hamilton will be looking forward to meeting you."
And I, meeting him.
"Mr. Bilsky you are the nicest person I have spoken to all day."
Thank you, you're nice too.
"Thank you, have a nice day."

And the line went silent.

I sat back smiled, and began to wonder –
Which one of my relatives will call me, For a short loan over a long period?

I can hardly wait to see what's in tomorrow's mail –

P.S. "I was asked if I would want to subscribe to TV weekly."
I said I already have one to use, as our condo association has one available, if we want one.
She said – "Oh, that's good."

Moses Bilsky

WHO ARE YOU?

Maxamillius was supercilious,
　　But didn't know his front from his back
So when he left he was Joseph –
　　And on the way back he was Jack.

Sometimes he was discouraged,
　　Defeat was his middle name.
Until his wife encouraged him,
　　And winning became his game.

Most days he complained of being tired,
　　But not due to lack of sleep.
It was always a fight and a struggle –
　　And a sense of loving, to keep.

So Joseph went down and jack went up
　　The proverbial Hill of Life.
And fought the Battle of Jericho,
　　To the sound of drum and fife.

"I won", he cried, at the top of the hill –
　　And my name is Jack forever.
So tomorrow at light of day,
　　I'll take time to pray.

And thank God – I know who I am.

MORAL – Fight longer and harder – Stay Alive!

Six Feet Tall, Three Feet Short

THINK NOW

I wish today was yesterday –
  Because I had wished for a better day.
But got today.
  Maybe I didn't wish hard enough.
I'll try again tomorrow.

NOTE:
  The space between "Mobility" and "Stability"
  Depends upon my balance and Determination.

My favorite title for my next writing:
  "Agony – in the Belly of the Pit"

Careful – don't trip on the following –
  Attention – Suspension – Prevention – Detention

Why, do we ask and wonder Why?
  When we can find out Because.

Hazardous – Horrendous – Stupendous – Tremendous
Ask your friends if they know the only four words in the dictionary ending
in "Dous" – You're smarter then they are!

DEFINITIONS

STROKE – Boxed in a confined area, bound by limitations of mobility,
and exhaustion, none of which are by your choosing.

LOVE – You can't see it, feel it, or explain it – But you know it. The power
of one, magnified by two.

Moses Bilsky

REMEMBERING

Have you ever heard the slap of a Beaver's tail
    Or the cry of a lovesick Loon
Or watch a pale moon climb –
    Amongst pine trees
Around a secret hidden lagoon?

Perhaps you've seen the minnows play,
    In clear water on a sandy shore
When out in deeper depths they wait
    For a cast of plug, hook, and more.

The excitement of pull and jerk of the line
    And a yell "I Gotcha Now"
Completes with the scream of the reel
    With a bend in the rod, straight down.

The row back to camp
    With a smile and a thought –
That the day has been worth its while
    For a camp fire lit
    And a pine smoke smell
From a Barbecue's fire pit.

It's a young boy's thought
    In an old man's mind
So written now to remember
    Of days gone by – but still bright
Seeing places in bright moonlight.

Six Feet Tall, Three Feet Short

A SPECIAL THOUGHT

Do not cry this night for me –
    For it is I, who weeps for Thee.
This strange day of mixed emotion
    Does not advance the foolish notion –
That I would leave this life
    Before saying goodbye –

To those I love,
    And have yet to meet,
One who could take the place –
    Of my most precious mate.

Who alone can stand
    Against all odds,
Of being God's Greatest Gift,
    A partner with no equal.

Who measures love with her eyes
    And care with her heart.
With the stamina and strength
    Of a Thousand Angels.

To look after this appreciative soul.

Moses Bilsky

They say "Life is a bowl of cherries"
Who are THEY?
How big is the BOWL?
How many CHERRIES?

A 6 MINUTE THOUGHT –
Have you ever been in a group that left you restless – a little unhappy, and even sorry you accepted the invitation?

See if any of the about to be listed, reminds you of a night you regretted being involved in – so I tell this story:

So – I'm entertaining at dinner. And among my guests are:
Mrs. Everyone
Dr. Kook
Sara Beenthere
Judge Planner
    And
Chiquita Bananas
And as dinner was being served, we chatted about:
Betty Bobnose
Sally Tiptoe
Snott Dunnit
Well – let me tell you, it was a wild night.
Liquor mixed with Terra Sue, as desert was served.

Scotch coffee washed down the French Soufflé. And the floor was open to discussions.
"Who" sat next to me –
    And
"You" sat next to "You know what?"

We argued, yelled, dirty-eyed "them", and asked for clean napkins for the take-home leftovers.

The Chef came out and asked us –
"Please – don't come back."

Six Feet Tall, Three Feet Short

THE SILLINESS OF ME
In Honor of Jamie

The silliness of me,
  Is way beyond
  The foolishness of you.
Since I am committed
  By personal choice
And criticize you
  By public acclaim.

When others laugh
  At what they think I've done
It hurts, beyond being deep.
  For they know me naught
  And ought to be taught
Since I'm deprived of sleep

If I laugh at myself,
  And enjoy the sound –
Is it really right to be proud?

That you bring me to tears
  With little regard
When you point
  And laugh out loud.

Why not curb your tongue
  And leave me be
While I relish –
  At the silliness of me.

Moses Bilsky

FANTASY

I often wonder at what age in life
　　Do fantasy's come into play?
And whether they be real or not.
　　But at least in the mind or so I think
Are exciting and actual caught.

As a boy I don't remember,
　　A particular incident or wish.
That I would be a part of anything
　　Other than what I thought was normal
And pleasing to a purist's dish.

But as I grew up,
　　And supposedly knew life
I never needed un-played thoughts
　　For all thoughts of special excitement
Were always with my wife.

So now at eighty-four, the fun for me
　　Is comparing my medical history,
With those who also have aches and pains
　　And all kinds of stories and games.

I meet all kinds of people, friends, and neighbors too,
　　In my daily wheel around.
So now I collect stories,
　　That make a library bound.

There are those on canes and crutches
　　Whose hips replaced, don't work.
And some who pee each hour
　　And others have different quirks.
Fallen arches, squeaky knees
　　Elbows out of joint.

Six Feet Tall, Three Feet Short

Ears no longer listen, eyes that hardly see,
　　Balding hair, and missing teeth
They each and all –
　　Sound just like me.

So no matter where my pain is now
　　It's bound to move around.
Allowing me self sympathy
　　Before I hit the ground.

I'm forming my own private club
　　And inviting all who care
To join the midnight pee-pee group
　　The line forms to the right of the stair.

Don't be embarrassed by standing there
　　Pull up a chair, and wait
Find a reason to laugh at yourself
　　Before it becomes to late.

Moses Bilsky

AND THEN THERE IS ME

Idolized by Parents
Home safe from War
Well educated
Loved by wife
Adored by in-laws
Liked by friends
Admired in sales
Devoted Father
Successful in business
Hard working
Pianist, Artist
Motorcycle nut
Surrounded by comfort
Struggled and won
Serious surgeries
Stroke victim
Mostly healthy
Excellent tastes
Fair minded
Charitable
Giving
Religious
God Fearing

And at age 84
Mind if I Brag?

Six Feet Tall, Three Feet Short

SUB – ZERO

By the Grace of God, in his wisdom,
    I turned all of eighty-four today.
And bought ourselves a two-door ice-box
    A Sub – Zero, with lights, and bells and lock.
Now if anything is wrong, musical notes it plays
    And signals where in the manual
The answer for trouble lays.
    So somewhere between page 8, 10 or twelve
It's as plain as on your face,
    That now you must use an index
To describe the problem in place.

The manual has few pictures –
    And no trouble starter page.
But it does show the motor
    And gives outside dimension complete
And though it has an ice cube tray
    It's not making ice today.

But the lights go on – and the bells ring
    With payments not due 'till March
So we'll flip pages, and read and read
    While waiting for repairs
My vodka won't be quite as cold
    Nor will her scotch have frost
But enough from each bottle
    Will equate the overall cost
And by next March –
    Well –
All should be okay.

Moses Bilsky

THANKS DAD

Is a Boy's love – A Man's need?

Does he need me to mature, or do I need him to further my growth and understanding as a human being and as a Father?

I think I learned about love from my Mother. There is no stronger tie. But I learned about the fine points of life from my Father. I saw his delight in being the Head of the Household. My Father taught me about the principles of survival – I learned of my important existence through my Mother.

But my mindful thoughts, especially private, were Man's. Being able to reach certain goals were my bragging right to share with my Father. Secrets with or about family were traded because – just because. But special happenings could best be explained to my dad – no questions asked – no tears – no apologies – just private talks.

My Father was a special image. A door that was always open – always understanding – never accusatory – and always reachable.

I had few treasured moments in time that were for Men only – Moments that were necessary masculine – treasured moments that carried the feelings of a secret trust – laughable moments that could only be enjoyed between Father and Son – understandable moments only to be shared by two – not three – not family….. just a moment between He and Me.

They were not frequent – but I remember them far better – much clearer – more decisive – than growing up in a loving home. It was never one – never both –

Six Feet Tall, Three Feet Short

It was just a couple of boys – needing to be men – and sharing men's moments – whatever that might be. I grew up knowing my father's image was within me, with a special love, knowing that no one else would understand – and I would not need to explain it – ever.

If only I could have one more moment with my Dad –

And now I, the writer – want one more moment with my son –

LEGACY

I am my Father's Son -
    And as such
Carry my name with pride.
    So that all must see and know,
How years, and days and deeds
    Allow no fact to hide.

It's a Family trait.

And thus I live with the one I love,
    And trust beyond compare
To raise our children,
    So they can share – a legacy
With honor – without fear –
    Of looking back,
And excitement, expecting tomorrow.

They too – can say He was my Father,
    And my Mother at his side.
They always gave breath to out existence
    And we in turn shall do likewise.
For ours.

Moses Bilsky

CAN YOU HEAR ME

Why do we wonder
  About everything?
And do nothing about most.

Is it possible we don't care,
  To interfere with the course –
Of Life, over which no control –

Seems the passive course and,
  Appears to be the easiest.

I watch from above –
  To those below,
And wonder just when to intrude.
  Should I voice out loud,
  Or allow a cloud,
To shadow a wrong to proceed.

It's midnight now,
  With 'morrow to come –
I have time to think of my action.
  With concern for right from wrong –
And speak, or act, or cry out.

Will anyone listen, Will anyone care?

Six Feet Tall, Three Feet Short

LOST FEELING

I'm lost in a wash of worry
    And can't seem to settle my mind.
With commitment made to surgery -
    God only knows what they'll find.

I beg them don't play diagnoses
    With lantern to light the way.
Don't dilly and dally, and poke and prod
    Just get in and get out
    And leave no doubt
I'm not going under the sod.

Enough about me –
    Let's talk about you

And the constant struggle to survive
How brave you are, and the strong must be.
    Each moment of thought –
    To staying alive.

I understand that weakened smile
    And a constant tear in the eye.
Been there, done that, and holding my breath to pray
    In hopes that all might be –
A chance, A hope, for another day.

Moses Bilsky

TOTAL NONSENSE

What difference does it make –
    In the way I write.
As long as you notice
    It rhymes at night.

I don't have a thought,
    Since I often flip-flop,
And talk about things unexplored
    When I play shuffle board.

Or perhaps I duke,
    With a guy named Luke.
Who's blood is a flood.
    So what – he's a dud.

And that I love Paris
    When I drive my Polaris.
To meet Harry –
    Sitting up for Harri-Karri.

I'm really quite heavy,
    As I drive my new Chevy.
And weave in and out,
    When I start to pout.

So always the achiever,
    Never the aggriever.
I work like a beaver,
    When I handle cleaver.

Six Feet Tall, Three Feet Short

SPIDER

Our hold on life is by a thread.
    It gets thinner by each day.
But we hold on tight as the spider spins,
    And captures moments and hours.
With a drag, a slough, or wheelchair push,
    In the direction of "survival".
With the mask of "smiles".

I know some who don't want to continue
    And what a waste that thought must be.
Not wanting to breathe, and try once more.
    My GOD – just open the door.
Find out what's out on the other side –
    To the secret of life –
    Respect the "gift" that is yours to control.
And carry on, for the one you love –
    And for those your responsibilities always flow.

You have the privilege of life –
    And the responsibility of sharing with others.
It's not a rule, but a common prayer,
    Which lies within us –
    Silently.
Allowing our spider to spin a thread to tomorrow.

Moses Bilsky

A PERSONAL MOMENT

Shhhhh---- Listen, I think the winds are playing our song.
    The melody is so soft –
And the crispness of Fall is in the air.
    Look – only one dandelion waves its' yellow hue.

There – there's quiet in the air.
    And the wet leaves are starting to cover next year's blooms.
Thank GOD we're able to see forever together.

But all that we think, as mentioned before,
    Is only a figment of imaginations.
And our time has not come –
    To warmly rest together.

I pray for you –
    As you do for me.
And were blessed with being alive today
    And capable of enjoying extra moments of life –
What blessings we possess.

Our family, surrounded in up-righteous togetherness
    With protective spirit for each other -
And knowledge that -
    All for one - and one for all
Is the code of honor, each bares with pride.

Six Feet Tall, Three Feet Short

A RESTLESS MIND

I grieve for those who no longer grieve.
    And shed a tear for they who cannot cry.
Although when necessary, I also pray for a power to be.
    When a power for me – allows me,
To cry, and grieve, far into the unknown night.

And daylight awakens to the sounds
    Of a restless mind –
A sound emits from the splash of the tear.
    And the lesson begins in the hours to come.
That one cannot carry the burden of responsibility –
    Without the knowledge and heart of the reason.

Know that when needed to count, be counted upon.
    Know too, that one tear – bespeaks of heartbreak;
    Crying – a time that will pass;
And grieving – just a moment in time.

How fortunate for those who can tell time beyond the clock's face. And have the patience to pray for a better tomorrow – And wipe away the sadness of today.

Moses Bilsky

DATES REMEMBERED

OCTOBER 2007
Way back in November,
    I think I remember –
That doctors knew.
    0hat turned out to be true.
That a serious battle.
    To survive –
Was a choice,
    To staying alive.

The choice was not mine.
    Not really –
If I wanted to enjoy tomorrow.
    Sign the consent form today –
Allowing the nightmare
    To begin.

October vanished into November,
    Quickly swallowed up by December.
Allowing tests and treatments
    To get back,
    On track.
With one exception.

JANUARY 1, 2008
Treatment necessary –
    So different, it defies imagination
And in time,
    Calls for scheduled appointments
With a *Blue Ghost*
    Destined for healing
And unspeakable to explain.

So crushing my wife's hand in mine
    The solution is instilled within,
And all treatment for hours
    Depends upon hope, and the blue ghost – NURSE!

Six Feet Tall, Three Feet Short

Actually – paper protected – covered
 Head to toe, front and back,
 Gloved, masked, and a steady hand –
 Depending on gravity and prayer.
And another half hour fills the room with profanity, tolerable pain and hope.

JANUARY 1, THROUGH THE 18TH
 Four down – Two to go.
So I go along with theories –
 Especially those with series
That privilege harbors responsibilities.
 And thus I am lucky –
That cancer was timely discovered,
 And treated, and tolerated,
And leaving me able –
 To explain, handle, and laugh.

JANUARY 25TH AND THEREABOUTS –
I try to think – and imagine about time:
 Waiting – For what?
 Wasting – Why Worry?
 Wanting – Need more?
 Working – With a purpose?
 Thinking – About what?
Well in the first place, I thought,
 If I could see a sunset on this side of the mountain,
Instead of just the tail end – Would it be more beautiful?

With only one more procedural treatment to endure, the waiting, preys on ones mind. I watch the calendar. I count the days – no – 240 hours – 14,400 minutes – during which I think positive – negative – victorious, defeated, dejected, rejected – smiling – crying – happy – worried – and sensitive to all and every emotion possible. I so not know what tomorrow brings – but I do know that the unknown and unanswerable is the greatest scare and fear imaginable.

So I, with bated breath, now wait for **2/4/08**
For the last treatment for me medically, and wonder if I have prayed hard enough for God, and loud enough for the world to say –
Oh, what the Hell – let's give the old man the benefit of the doubt, cure him, love him, and let him enjoy a wee bit longer with family and friends.
Why not – maybe he can help somebody else get though a tough place in their life.

THE END -
Or is it?

Six Feet Tall, Three Feet Short

THINKING BACK – NOT BACKWARD THINKING

30 SECOND FLASHBACKS

Canadian born, 1923 Enjoyed real winters - snow angels, skated 5 miles on great canal, big houses, summers in North woods. Winter, cut ice from frozen lake, for summer storage in ice house – played in piles of sawdust. Great times at Aunts' estate and chauffer taking us out on private lake in special Gar Wood speed boat.

First piano lessons in kindergarten. Mother playing "In a Monastery Garden" on her European Steinway Piano. Beautiful to hear. Mother very proper, snobbish, straight, loving, always right. Father the gentleman, wore Hamburg hat, chamois gloves. Early years, Department Store Manager, buyer for fine sterling and diamonds, one of 13 children. Pushed around by rich relatives. His father, Moses Bilsky, an adventurer, married late in life, first prominent Jew in Canada, Fine Jeweler, I am namesake, Synagogue in family home.

Pesach – Passover, best Jewish Holiday I liked. Mother set Seder table in best china and silver – But Pink Ainsley China reserved for 1st place setting for Messiah for 1st night Seder. Attended Synagogue with regularity. Women in Balcony – Men on 1st floor. Boring or giggles. Kept looking up counting light bulbs in chandeliers so as not to sleep.

Our housed – big – 4 floors. In winter my job was to bank the coal in furnace for the night. Ice box has outside door on porch for delivery. I remember vestibule, formal parlor, music room, living-family room, dining room, butler's pantry, kitchen and back porch all on 1st floor.

Public piano lessons at school in kindergarten. Private one hour @ $1.00 when I was 14. Sometimes cheated, used lesson money for Saturday double-feature plus 3 serials movie. Admission .35 cents - Avalon cigarettes .11 cents a pack, candies etc. .03 to .08 cents variety. Had to smoke entire pack with friends before going home to report my progress at music lesson.

Came to States in 1935 – Chicago South Shore Hebrew Congregation, Rabbi Teller. Bar Mitzvah hated studying Hebrew and Yiddish. Learned to read and write both. Had to write letter in Yiddish, never knew to

Moses Bilsky

whom or why – even to this day. An unhappy experience. Said so at Bar Mitzvah dinner at Congress Casino - all relatives from Canada present. Mother caught breath and wanted to die. Father stood his ground saying he wasn't sure what he heard.

Louisville - Jr. High School. Dated twin sisters, liked the second one better than the first, changed in midstream. Names Sarah Jane and Sarah Jean. Forgot which was which. Both good bodies but not allowed to touch.

Several summers spent at Neporsit, Long Island, N.Y. Charles, the Butler in charge of all the cousins present. Exposed to art, music, etiquette, culture (whatever that is) in New York. In the city lived on the entire 15th floor of the St. Regis Hotel. It was the Canadian family's headquarters in the U.S.

Schools, Universities – B.A. Law Schools LLB & JD, Special Ohio University degree in Wholesale Management. While student and also studying art, employed part time as law clerk for powerhouse Law Firm. Prosecuted for Boss, Pendegast and O'Malley (whose partner was H.S.T. – later to be President of U.S.) I was court artist.

3 years winning World War II. One of General Patton's tank drivers. Drove 1st American tank across the Danube – not blue. 1st American tank force in the Metz - drove in and through a Department Store (my guys loved shopping that way). Was in Crailsheim when 1st attack of German jet planes were known to fly. History of air war about to change – then a charge to Bastone to relieve 101st airborne, and relieve we did, had a Hot Turkey Christmas dinner. Some guys' made money from German souvenirs, some shooting dice or playing cards – I did the safe thing – my mother each week sent me assorted salad dressings. The guys in the Battaleon stole vegetables from gardens – placed in steel helmets, with my salad dressing at $5.00 a pop.

Six Feet Tall, Three Feet Short

WWII

By the end of the war had accumulated over $15,000, in bonds sent home. Wife's father knew I had a small nest egg in which to marry his daughter - European War ended - I volunteered for Japan & Pacific Duty. 30 day furlough landing in N. Y. Harbor August 15, 1945 V.J. Day, soon discharged. War is and was Hell. Glad to be safe.

Continued education – Bar Exam – two attempts – Law License issued 1950. Started to work for my Father in Liquor Packaging Supplies, Had 17 lines to represent – only one customer.

Moving right along - met the Girl – dinner at Shangrila. Liked her, and promised to call – one year later, I did. 2nd date together was in Louisville – fell in love – 12 dates later got married, in 3 month span. She had horse and car – I had horse and car. We started life, with 3 bedroom home on ½ acre – 2 cars, 2 horses, lots of love and trust. Still true after 52 years together – same girl, plus 3 great kids.

Worked for my Father - them Father-in-law, then had 12 separate careers. Each one different. Sales rep, Women's Fashion Manager, Motorcycle Dealership, Furniture Sales. Time period of 48 years earning a buck or two also included Temporary Help, Office Personal, Real Estate, Apartment Rental Management, Banking , Private Investment Manager, Wholesale Automotive Parts Supplier and maybe a few I've since forgotten – anything to pay the family bills. One job even supplied a new T-Bird (red & white) and a 32 foot Yacht. By the way – all three babies were born during periods of unemployment.

I remember Barbeques on Sundays – lots of relatives just happening to drop by at the right time to begin with cocktails. My favorite career was a Honda Motorcycle Dealership in 1962 before car. Took 1 year old son for a cycle ride on highway strapped in front of me. Went on Eden's Highway. He liked the wind to pucker up his cheeks. Oh, oh passed grandparents on highway doing 65 mph. Promised never again - after all – in-laws owned our house.

Wore leather and boots everywhere. Full leather thought to be Porno oriented – so what – certainly a true safety factor.

Wife and I liked all things the same as each other. So being together gave us enjoyment and fun free time.

Late retired years, 2004 hit by stroke. Partial recovery and partial paralysis. Certainly slowed me down. Hurt my musical ability and crippled me. My greatest love in life - now also my caretaker.

Just stated writing to tell stories in 2006. No public outlet at this time. Working with the Rehab Institute to tell my story and prove there are still things one can do to teach - entertain & enlighten and prove untapped abilities.

Whatever the physical problems encountered, there are ways to compensate mentally, and learn to try – to go on, and accomplish new goals and levels of contentment.

My favorite medical prescription – Scotch or Vodka and sex if possible.

Six Feet Tall, Three Feet Short

Love strong, play fair, trust partner, share whatever you have, breathe deep, sleep well, and hope tomorrow comes.

NOTE: each aforementioned fact or sentence is a complete story in itself. Available in LEATHER BOUND 3 VOLUME SERIES. Advance deposit required, No Freebies.

Moses Bilsky
Wheelchair Truth

Moses Bilsky

LOOKING FORWARD TO NEXT YEAR

One moment, one minute, one step – perhaps one day, one life.

Each happy, healthy, sick, terrorized, filled with dreams into eternity, or totally blank. All encompassed by a hospital stay, filled with doctors, nurses, staff, aids statements, opinions, sleep, nightmares, discomfort, pain, relief, and mountainous thoughts of past present, future.

Of lights, darkness, silence, sounds, needles, pills, heart beats, pressure readings, tests, gurneys, machines, plates, film, food, ice, sips of water.

Thus for the past 30 days, all of the above occurred. I'm now home – with oxygen – love and a little energy – Than God for God!

Happy Hanukkah
Happy Holidays
Happy New Year
And to all a Good Life!

Marcia & Moe 2007

ZORRO 2/13/08

Zorro

It's a sad, dark, bleak beautiful sunny day. It's the middle of the week, and we lost a friend – loyal, tiny, loving, trusting, playful, obedient, caring, going blind, deaf, almost toothless, companion, snuggler, well-groomed, perfect family member.

His name is Zorro. Not was but is Zorro. We rushed him to our Vet, but found it would be necessary to make the ultimate last decision – sleep – forever - no suffering, or whimpering, or struggling. Just sleep – and forever remain in our thoughts, and memory of one we cherished, idolized, adored, and always comforting, warm and wiggled into our affections.

The sun was bright. Our hearts are dark; tears stream - dry-up – and stream again.

Zorro – one of a kind, perfect friend – we'll miss you – think of you, and know you're now having comfort where ever you might be playing through eternity.

Wednesday, half way here, half way there. Always in our hearts and mind. Thanks for being our friend.

Moses Bilsky

INBETWEEN

It's the middle, of the middle of the night.
    Yet I remember and recall yesterday
And hopefully look forward to tomorrow
    And although I remember no sin,
    For which I would apologize –
I am sorry for not having accomplished
    More, during my time among
    Friend or foe.

With all the heartfelt love I hold within
    I have only shared it with those –
    Closest to my kind-
And I am bothered by not really understanding
    What is, or are, my so – called kind.

So if knowingly I stay in-between each choice.
    Am I entitled, and allowed to manipulate
    My mind for the goodness of deed.
To penetrate the importance of necessary
Sharing of fairness, love, protection and
    Helpfulness to those who need,
    To those who want,
    To those deserving, and,
    To those who share.
I remain here at the discretion of the
    Almighty Power
I remain here to accomplish a love –
Sharing wish –
    I remain here as a purposely,
    Child of GOD

Six Feet Tall, Three Feet Short

IN THE MIDDLE

Is this the beginning of the end, or perhaps the end of the beginning? I am sure however, that life, somehow, always completes a cycle. And therefore, we should each find pleasure and happiness between joy and tears. Is that what was meant, when we stood before all, and promised in sickness and health, for richer or poorer. Do we find that those words reverberate with more severity, the older, perhaps wiser we get – clears, when we examine closer, and softer, when we love in return for love? How lucky we are when we say in complete honesty – Been there – done that – wish I could do it all over again - the same.

CELEBRATION

I'm not there with you. But I'm here with you. I've known Virginia since 1956 when she was my down the street neighbor.

I still know her as one of my best friends. We had a means of communication that knew no limits, no barriers, and no equal.

What can I say – Virginia – your comments on each of my writings, give me the courage
to write what I think and feel, and your silent applause, to allow me to think that I am able to stand aside from my wheelchair and applaud you in return.

How fortunate I have been to meet you, know you, understand you, and in the excitement of life, know we will meet – someplace – sometime and hold dear the friendship which we treasure for all time.

Written for a dear friends wife to be read at the memorial service May 4 2008

Moses Bilsky

TOMORROW'S ORDER

It's the other side of midnight.
    And I am where I usually am –
At the desk-
In the dark –
Alone with my thoughts.
There's no dog that barks.
The City sleeps.
    And I rule the World – and –
    In full control of my destiny.

And if all of the above –
    Are true.
Why don't I change everything –
    To my way.
Remove sadness,
All in Good Health –
    Poverty – to vanish,
    Wars to end.
    (They're really Hellish)
Kindness, politeness, and manners –
    To be the name of the game.
Not guns –violence, hatred, or lies,
And fairness, with politics to better, -
    And justice really for all.
    With friendships polished – not tarnished,
    With Laws to serve – not varnished.
I, in my tower of loneliness
    In conjunction, with my God – I,
Ask only one thing in prayer.
    That all be well.
    And each newborn,
        Be allowed to live –
        In peace. -

Six Feet Tall, Three Feet Short

ABOVE AND BEYOND

Beyond my infancy,
    Yet-
Prior to my demise,

I have places to see,
Friendships to share,
A woman to love,
Children to idolize,
A full life to enjoy,
    And to share with –
Those who wish and want
    And think and understand.
    To love –
With whom to listen
    And sing,
    And hear.

And the list goes on –
    As does the Beat of Life.

How lucky I am to hear –
    Even as tired as I might be.
My wife – my love –
My inspiration, and heart,
    And beat of life.

All signal there is still tomorrow.
    Look forward to it –
And hope Prayer and love
    Carries you through –

One more gracious Day. 3:10 AM

Moses Bilsky

If you're not sure if you're coming or going
Try hither or yon OR up and down.

NO – NEVERMIND –
I'LL JUST SIT HERE ALONE AND CRY

I think it's a case of sad wonderment,
  To be in a corner alone – and say –
Just go ahead without me –
  I won't be able to keep up anyway.

It's really too hard to even try,
  As the blur of life flies by
Perhaps I'll just feel sorry for me –
  All I want is to be free!

From What?

Well let me tell you from what!

Are you interested in not breathing?
  Try it.
Keep those you love at arms length!
  Who will it hurt?
Give up mobility!
  Stop moving.
If you don't go –
If you don't push –
If the wheels stop –
Is there nothing to see?
Is there nothing to learn?
Nothing else to experience?
Can it all be over?
  Because you think it is?

Not so with some of the people I saw today –
  They can't talk –
  They can't express –

Six Feet Tall, Three Feet Short

Their head won't stay up –
Eyes won't focus –
Can't move – can't transfer –
Can't stand – can't sit straight.
    In particular
I saw someone – who has to lie back –
    So far, that only his head,
    Is at level of his hips.
    With legs and feet being –
    3 feet straight up.

Everyone has a purpose,
    To be alive this day,
    To exist.
Sure I cried. Not for me.
But for those who know
    How lucky I am.

BE IT KNOWN

The greatest gift of Heritage Is the independence of the Child from the father. –
And Success is knowing who, and what you are, and being satisfied with your accomplishment, – Regardless of their acceptance by society or your Neighbor.

Moses Bilsky

REFLECTIONS OF A TIRED MIND

For the rest of my Life –
I will never stand unaided.
    Get in a bathtub - Stand at a bar.
    Stand in a line - Drive a car.
Or do a thousand other things
    But I live, and love, and see,
    And listen, and enjoy –
A thousand other things –

AN IRRESISTIBLE THOUGHT – FROM AN IRRESPONSIBLE MIND.

It's a quarter past midnight,
    And all are asleep.
Except for me –
    And revelers on the street.

And I, in my most triangulated view of me – reflects only what I want to see. Not that which is actual, or within view of my blinded vision. Perhaps I should put my glasses on. Am I to correct all of the wrongs around me? Are my thoughts and words strong enough to make a difference?
    I hope so. –
Striking when the iron is hot – might burn you –
    Think twice before using.

If I am an endangered species, will the Government protect me forever?

Six Feet Tall, Three Feet Short

WHO? - ME WHY – BECAUSE
WHEN – NOW
WHERE – HERE WHAT – WHO?

WOODCHUCK IN THE WILLOW

"Talk to me" the Willow said, as it gently swayed in the breeze. Tell me of the Trials and Tribulations you experience, and perhaps I can help you help yourself.

"But I'm not the problem" replied the Woodchuck –
It's just that so much is expected of me –
That I get totally exhausted chucking wood,
Just because some people want to know,
How much wood could I chuck, if I could chuck wood?

Well – perhaps your answer lies in chucking less than expected, and more than actually needed.

And that's like I asked you "Why do you weep?"
Regardless of breeze or storm? Don't you tire unnecessarily if you keep moving just because?

We'll – "Perhaps we should make a pact" to always be available when needed and be still when not. And you work to the best of your ability, giving more than expected. And a little less, so there is no waste of energy.

"Agreed" "Agreed".

And the gnawing could be heard round the world –
In the soft compelling billowing of the clouds –
As the winds rolled across the heavens.

Enough said – Think about it – Proof.
What Goes Around, Comes Around.

First attempt for Children only

Moses Bilsky

LIFE

For all you old asses-
    When you read,
S, with 3 dashes
    It doesn't spell S-A-F-E.

'Cause the idea of "disgust"
    I'm sure that it must,
Have stronger meaning than 'that'.

It feels like –
And sounds like –
And I'm sure that it is.

Just plain, old, and descriptive –
Of what life really is.

Six Feet Tall, Three Feet Short

A.M. – MAYBE?

OB – SLOB
    Rebeca – Da' Moor
DA Hoop Deloop
    DA shall de' More.

Cheering for what –
    I did not know
Crying with tears
    After all those years.

Of living, working
    And wondering why
The evil in life
    Exists on high –
While the poor,
    Barely survive.

Yet the balance between
    Never seems to meet.

The young grow old
    The tired grow weak
I know what should be –
    If wishes could speak.

The world would make sense
    If we all spoke French –
With kisses and wine,
    So that all would be fine.

After dinner – that is!

I write these at 3:00
Cause I get up to Pee.

Moses Bilsky

"LILLY LOVELY"

Timmy Lumber –
    Picked a number –
His favorite was twenty – six

But at thirty – one
    He had just begun
To realize LIFE could be fun.

With marriage to learn about living
    Allowing independence, and burden free.
And perhaps to think about family –
    Maybe as many as three.

There were Good Times, and bad –
    Some happy, some sad,
With hard, and tough in-between.
    But always each seemed perfect
    Through out the years
    Even with multiple tears
So that each day was worthwhile
    Because of her smile.

No wonder they call her "Saint Lilly"

She knew it, she did it –
    No task was to hard
Her family important –
    Even cutting the yard.

Through fifty – four years – We were graced by God.
    To be loved by each other –

There is no end to this story.

Six Feet Tall, Three Feet Short

PERSONAL CHALLENGE

Cream Puffs and icicles
    Are on the menu today –
Where Eskimos, Laplanders and children play.

It's cold – It's fun – and the game is fair
    The Elders don't cheat
When they all come to meet.

And so it is also
    In the heat down south
Perhaps the reason - might be a drought.

But across the world
    It all seems the same
When your down and out, you play without shame.

If you win – your lucky.
    If you lose there's no shame.
But if you tried your damnedest
    That's your doorway to fame.

The key is you tried
    And announce to all.
"I will if I can"
    It was mine to call.

Win – Lose – or break even,
    It had my best effort
Before thinking of leave'n.

Moses Bilsky

MIDNIGHT ROAMER

Roaming the house after midnight
    Is an experience indeed.
'Cause you look for the "not necessary"
    And seek "Above and beyond"
The "Call of necessity".

Bathroom privileges are allowed –
    And routines there –
    Are the same.

But the adventure begins,
    Once down the hall –
Beyond earshot – and light flash
    It's a big shopping mall.

There's a place called "Refrigerator Heaven"
    Where left-over's are a-plenty.
And near by, is an open Bar.
    For a wee Sherry – and Tiny Tar-Tar.

Then past a closet,
    Though hard to reach
Has this – and that –
    With salt, and sweet.
Stored in little jars –
    Keeping all very neat.
And then back to the freezer
    For a Cool-Whip Treat.
Just because it's there,
    And can be reached from my chair.

Six Feet Tall, Three Feet Short

And then through space and time,
I'm at the desk –
To remind you, my Reader –

"I'm back" – I'm back"
To tell all again –
"Good Morning Friend"

It's Five A.M.

JUST IN TIME – A RHYME

If I had the wings of an Angel,
    As silly as it might seem –
I'd fly around the world, and try,
    To justify, and understand –
Chaos, poverty, sickness and war.

If it didn't make sense and –
    There is a cure.
With my magical powers
    All would be pure –

And right – in the World.

Goodness Gracious
    Sakes alive.
How I've managed
    To stay alive.

Live right –
    Play hard
Keep an eye
    On the North Star.

And Know –
    Your direction in Life.

Moses Bilsky

SOMEONE

I wonder if you, or –
    Anyone!
Knows how deep,
    The depth of Despair
Can drag the Human Mind?

Is there a bottom?
    Where one can level out,
And climb –
    Or at least begin
To rationalize.

What to hold on to,
    In order to begin –
The ascent to the starting point.
    Of yesterday,
Or perhaps yesteryear.

If a Blessed Helping Hand
    Can be reached –
    Or even touched –
Grab – Hold tight.
    It's a momentary flash,
Which lights the way –
    To salvation, and the
    Revelation –
That this is the one moment in time.

In which the Heavens open –
    The light brightens,
    And shines on that one person
    With hand outstretched –
Call Him – or Her
    FRIEND.

LIFE IS A GAMBLE

Ya know, I used to be –
    I'm sure I was,
And maybe, I still am –

A tough Road Hog,
    And leather clad
Braggadocios, S.B., old sod –
    Highways, and Byways
Knew no bound
    Just Wind and Speed –
Flashed above the ground.

It wasn't the Devil,
    That made me do –
It was just because I wanted –
    What nobody else could do.

And so it has been
    Through most of my life,
I have to be on top,
    So I could brag,
And boast of course,
    I even had a horse.

I'd sell whatever came to hand,
    Be it product, service, or thought,
And I worked for the highest bidder –
    So it was true, I could be bought.

But when it came to family –
    I paid what ever price,
Was necessary, to keep us all
    United, together,
For the roll of the dice.

Moses Bilsky

THOUGHTS BEFORE THINKING

Eighty – Five!
 My God –
I'm still alive.

Trying to reach –
 Six, Seven or Eight.
Might be a big mistake.

It depends upon
 Quality.
 Mobility,
Certain utility
 And the facility,
And the purpose -
 Of my mind!

So again, late – late – late –
I make notes in order
Not to forget.

Like:
Titles Of Books I Own.
(Which I am not going to write.)

1. Somewhere, On The Other Side Of Nowhere.
2. Why Tomato Soup Always Taste Like Tomatoes.

Facts I Have To Live With –

A. Can a short story be written with one word? Try!
B. If tomorrow is "crucial" – are we on edge today?
C. Doctors, greeting you on the first visit, wearing a glove and a smile.
D. Elevators which will go sideways, when you don't know the address.
E. While I'm "at it" – Why not "finish it"!
F. World Peace – May I – Can I – Really help?
G. With the name of "MOSES" – I should be able to –
AT LEAST TRY.

Six Feet Tall, Three Feet Short

THOUGHTS – AFTER THINKING

I'm sorry –
    And I know not why
'Cause I think, and know
    I really try.

To lead the way of life –
    As taught by my Father
    By His Father
And to know today,
    It was the right way.

So I'm able to show,
    And proud to explain
The seed which I've sown
    Down a Bright shady lane.

That led to an accomplished life
    Of unbelievable surprises.
Including a WAR of tears and strife,
    And then a salesman's life
With a special prize.

The Best of all –
    The Lady I married
Who stays with me yet
    Allowing Odds on a bet.

After Fifty – Four years

I Win - I Win - I Win!

Moses Bilsky

MEANINGFUL WORDS

When in College –
    Perhaps High School – or grammar
Discipline was self evident –
    And the only choice was "do"
Coupled with "Learn" and "Respect"
    Life had an automatic flow –
And whether summer heat
    Met winter snow,
We grew up thanking yesterday –
    And excited for tomorrow.

Now the un-sureness of the day,
    And worries about pay –
Cause struggle and strife,
    And lead one through
An unsure life.

But this Holiday weekend,
    During which I write
Gives me great cause to worry,
    Regarding Life and Wife.

Surgery scheduled –
    To remove Cancer once more,
Number Four!

Lucky – I pray – I hope – I cry!
    One more time – one more day,
To come back, and be able to say.

I love you,

And say it – every chance I get!

Six Feet Tall, Three Feet Short

AGAIN – AGAIN AND AGAIN

I'm always looking, for things to write,
    On everything wrong, that I can right.

But this time I'm fooled –
    A missed diagnostic tool.
That my cancer was gone –
    So my life would be long.

On Wednesday last, my tests were past
    So I celebrated –
    With six days of freedom.
But yesterday, with correction made –
    By telephone – was startling news –
An oversight was told:
    "We're sorry"
My cancer – no longer on hold.

I cried – I screamed –
    Why now – How come!
    Where do I turn –
    What's next. –
I can only see hope,
    In the tears of my wife.
And know that some how –
    I'll go on with my life.

So we're lining up tests
    And telling those who care,
That we'll steel ourselves again –
    To the rigors of pain.

Moses Bilsky

And the suspense –
    And the prayers –
And hope through despair
    That the fight
    Though constant –
Has to be fought with a goal.
    That survival after all,
    Is in the depth –
Of our soul.

With family beside,
    And treatments planned –
God helps me once more.
AND CANCER BE DAMNED!

Six Feet Tall, Three Feet Short

QUICK – SAY

'Twas the night before surgery
    With my mind running wild –
And wall shadows everywhere
    Had reflections of a child.

+++++++++++++++++++++++

My Mother knew –
    Tuck it in the corset,
Tuck it in the Bra.
    It might not be the right place,
But it was good enough for Ma.

It didn't pay interest,
    With availability to none
But always there when needed
    To share with everyone.

+++++++++++++++++++++++

Fool me once –
    And never again,
'Cause your second chance –
    Is gonna give you pain.

+++++++++++++++++++++++

In my Mother's kitchen on the wall
    A Shakespeare plate announcing to all –
"There's a saying old and musty,
    Yet 'tis always ever new,
'Tis never Trouble Trouble –
    Till trouble troubles you"

+++++++++++++++++++++++

Two prunes eaten at 4:00 A.M.
    Showed up
@ 11:08A.M.
    I felt so good
I took a nap.

Moses Bilsky

IT'S IMPORTANT

Today, I'm eighty –five
     But feel like sixty – two.
And the best of all the years,
     Were spent in loving you.

It wasn't just a roll in the hay –
     Or a gallop down the trail.
But the quality times,
     Spent talking
As the years together prevailed.

So let's –

     Do it again!

FOUR SEASONS

What I like about –

WINTER: Water in cold tap is really COLD.

SUMMER: Air conditioning.

FALL: Don't want to.

SPRING: No longer in my step.

Six Feet Tall, Three Feet Short

JUST NONSENCE

When the family of Questionables
    Meet the family of Positives
It's the Maybes wont try
    And the Must haves don't need.

++++++++++

Huff is to Puff,
    As
Tish is to Tosh –

++++++++++

Can you tell?
    Which is witch,
Without scratching –
    The itch?

++++++++++

Feature my TODAY, in headlines –
    Kiss my tomorrow, and be gone.
The fact is that NOW is important,
    And what might be. –
    Is maybe.
Who, is really NOW –
    And is worth all the future maybes –
And perhaps!

What if it's if?
    With the World in my palm,
I call the shots –
    And my knowledge,
Steers the course –
    Away from yesterday.

Moses Bilsky

IT'S OKAY

I have a close friend,
    And he's one of a kind.
So he only exists –
    In the corner of my mind.

He nothing like me –
    And certainly not you,
"Cause his two eyes are red,
    And the third one is blue.

But he can do stuff –
    If you truly believe,
When in the middle of the night
    He sits on my sleeve –
        And says –
        "NOW WHAT"?

This image, with one eye blue
    Kinda reminds me –
Of someone like you.
    But you're more gentle,
With a great big smile,
    And he has ears
Shaped like the Nile. –
    BUT HE LISTENS!

His name is Sir Safely –
    With a mind not too quick
But the love in his heart,
    Is the size of a brick.

And he laughs –
And he plays –
    As the day is long
He's a joy to be with
    When he sings his song.

Six Feet Tall, Three Feet Short

About us – and how we feel
   With words of truth,
   Which ooze with delight
When he hears that you've had
   A very good night.

And you awake, with a smile
   Though the day may be tough,
And he stretches God's Hand –
To guide you through rough.
   Hoping your safe –
In the morning sun.
   With enough strength
   To get through the day
   And be safe –
   In any way – Possible.
Even though the 'morrow,
Is just another day.

But with hope it will be better
   Or as good as today
Hope for it, Pray for it.
   Just wait and see
My friend Sir Safely
   Will save the day
And you will be just fine.

Moses Bilsky

A TRUE STORY? MAYBE

And God said unto MOSES –
    "Let there be light."

And Moses said –
    ("Whoops – where's das switch –?)
And there was light.

Dat's the way it was –
Dat's the way it is –
    And
Dat's the way it's gonna be.

Then God asked Moses –
    Why you walking in the desert
    without your bunny slippers?
Listen Lord – wait – I'll build a big boat,
    You make it Rain, and I'll save civilization.

We'll have a bunch of parties –
    Everybody can give speeches –
We'll print a bunch of money –
And see who can afford anything.

Once people have something –
    We'll take it right away from some,
    And end up with just rich and poor,
Everybody won't be able to afford anything,
    Some people will cheat each other
And all the people, except some will lose.

And Dat's the way it will be
    Believe it or not – So there.

Six Feet Tall, Three Feet Short

HUMPTY DUMPTY

My name is Humpty Dumpty
    And boy - did I have a fall.
Even though I answer to "Moses"
    The greatest name of all.

Nothing happens to me I'm sure,
    At normal times of the day,
But only when all are sleeping
    When mice come out to play.

From wheelchair, to walker -
    While backing up to you know where
I slipped -
And fell -
    While sound asleep
    And wedged between the chair -
        And tub.

A half hour of pull and tug
    We worked to no avail.
So 911 was dialed at last -
    And show up, they sure did,
And picked me up and turned me over
    Like a pot without a lid.

So to the chair and back to bed,
    And check for cuts and bruises,
They said "good night". I smiled and waved
    And prayed I don't have Twosys!

Moses Bilsky

THOUGHTS

1. It's important to make a decision at the end of your life - to know how important it was to make the right one at the beginning.
2. No lie is big enough to cover over the truth.
3. Truth belittles the least exaggeration.
4. A little white lie does not color a situation enough to make it palatable.

FIVE

I'm just beginning to realize -
    That I'm a number, and not a name,
For when I'm called or sequenced,
    A number comes before fame.

Years ago, I was drafted -
    And lined up by two's and four's
To be taught how to hurry and wait
    And only reveal 3569-8058.

But long before becoming a citizen
    A born Canadian, I certainly was -
And crossed the border in '35
    With a tender beard - really fuzz
And issued a number
    It ended in five.

Then passed by:
    School years - war years - law school.
    Single - married - family,
All referred to by,
    Numbers, letters, more numbers.
My lucky number is 5.

Everything was, is, and will be numbers.

Six Feet Tall, Three Feet Short

EASY AS PIE

An abundance of health issues,
    These past 25 years
Have been filled with physicians and surgeons
    And loaded with fears.

I've been lucky -
    Each time the knife plunged
And corrected a troubled spot -
    From hurting a lot.

Some ailments were original
    Some duplicated -
    Some complicated -
All surmountable -
    And each accountable -

But now - a third repeat,
    A must - do feat.
A knife - a steady hand,
    A prayer - a chance
It's as easy as pie -
    If you like pie.

And I "hope I go home."
    "With the lady what brung me."

We'll see?

Moses Bilsky

FIGHT

I'm about to fight
    A fight that is -
Fit to be fought
    As the fight of a lifetime.

It's my fight
    And the frightening enemy
        Is CANCER.

A formidable fighter -
    Without passion, or heart,
    Or sympathy -
And can last fifteen rounds
    With anger and pain.

After surgery in round seven -
    The fight is even.
But the Team in my corner -
    Well honed and trained -
    Full of love, and determination -
    Steered by fate -
Guided by my God -
    And the God of MOSES -

Will win this fight of fights.

So my cancer has returned with a vengence
    Unlike anything before
With a pain that surprised me
    And shivered me to the core.

Tough it out, the surgeon said -
    It's easier than being dead.

Six Feet Tall, Three Feet Short

And one night - a personal friend called -
    Told me to keep writing
    Beat my own drum.
    What's it matter if -
    They don't know where,
    I'm coming from.

Just do it -
    And tell it like it is.

WRITTEN

Once in memories, time lost -
    And so it should be as such.
By chance - in a moment to be forgotten -
    A hate spell, oozed from mind,
So sick.
    That death was inevitable
To quench it forever.

And so it was written,
    That only a viable love,
Could replace, cover and suppress,
    Future thought, though spiced -
And carried on the wind -
    To all four corners of mind and matter.

And each and all - would know
    That his call of
    "Yes we can" -
Held the spirit of future hope, For -
    All of the people, all of the time.

Not some - but all.
    And it was so heard.
And so it was written.

Moses Bilsky

FICTION & FACTS, FROM MOE'S ALMANAC

If you talk to yourself –
    Do you need an immediate answer,
    Or do you have time to think
    About it. –

Today my blood pressure is 110/70 – Great!
    Tomorrow – only the shadow knows.

It makes no SENSE
    To bespeak of nonsense –
Unless your desire for insistence,
    Leaves you insensitive.

I'm just a hard working woman –
    With a dust cloth in my hand.
So I swish and shwop –
    And push a mop –
But the work never ends.
    (You write the music, -
    I wrote the words)

If the pen is mightier than the sword –
    Why is everybody using a gun.

I WATCH

Only the falcon sees below
    Gliding a circle just above –
The circle of flight just flown.
    Smooth, surveying the majesty
Above and below.
    On wings of silence.

Six Feet Tall, Three Feet Short

I WOULD IF I COULD

If I think I'm so smart –
    'Cause I know how to fart,
And cover the fact
    With a smile.
You can be sure
    That I would –
If I thought that I could,
    But I can't.

Adversity seemed to
    Follow me,
While planning my future
    To make.
The old story prevailed
    Being a dollar short
Always entailed –
    The thought that I could,
But I can't.

So with hope
    For one day,
I'll be able to say –
    That Cancer
Is a thing of the past.

And at long, long, last
    With a vocabulary
So vast –
    That a Cystoscopy,
Is a word in Monopoly –
    And not a required must.

And I for one,
    Know that I could –
And did –

So there........

Moses Bilsky

TOMORROW

If you don't have a "Nickel to your name,"
    How can you turn "Around on a dime?"

I wonder –
    As I wander,
Through this cluttered
    Mind of mine.
How will I differentiate
    Importance,
That shivers the spine?

How can I possibly know
    When the corner is turned –
From the straight
    And narrow,
To the dangerous
    Curve ahead.
And eliminate,
    The precipice
Of despair –
    To the safe haven
Of sanity….

Courage seems to spring
    A resounding ring.
With trusted love
    The solid foundation.

How lucky a traveler
    Am I able to be,
That at eighty-six,
    I can see
The Rights from the Wrongs–
    The Good from the Evil,
Happy from Sad –
    And the lucky from Glad.

Six Feet Tall, Three Feet Short

Why – from why not,
 Do from Don't,
And lots of things,
 I know I forgot.

Why did I write this
 Late at night?
Because I was feeling,
 Sorry – for myself.
And what I want to say,
 This is my lucky day.
And I live –
 For tomorrow.

I WIN

Before you criticize
 The words that I make,
Be sure you know
 That I 'm wide awake.

I have a tendency
 To severely speak out
Before I know
 What it's all about.

Yet the fact remains
 When all's said and done
I'll keep on fighting
 Until I have won.

Moses Bilsky

NOW

Who among us
    Will stand and cheer?
And remember well,
    That I was here.

Who among you
    Will sing a praise?
While Brandy fills
    Our glasses raised.

Not just a name
    To remember well –
Since fleeting same
    Cast no spell.

Tell me now,
    Tell me how much.
Tell me why,
    I can feel your touch.

Hug me – kiss me –
    Just say goodbye.
You know I can't return,
    As hard I try.

Enjoy the moment –
    Hang on Tight.
Maybe we can get through
    One more night.

And if the morning shows
    I tried to stay –
The day starts now,
    Though I'm far away.

Dedicated to my friend
Joann DePinta

Six Feet Tall, Three Feet Short

AGAIN - ? – !

It's the shock of a life time
    When once again, appears
Tiny red globules,
    To heighten the fear,
That perhaps cancer –
    Is in mind and matter.

Comes a dash of Brandy
    At twelve – thirty AM
And the long wait
    Throughout the night
Of what might
    Or might not be.

The dreaded return
    Oh my worst enemy
Oh God – not again –
    Please –
Not again – Not again.

And we wait –
    And we watch,
And we wait –
    And we watch.

And we pray,
    It's the ultimate
Solution!

Five – Thirty seven A.M.
    All's clear –

Good Night –

Moses Bilsky

HUMPTY DUMPTY II

It's been a year of struggle and strife
    To maintain this peace looking life
When all the while – we cover the smile
    With falls, and tears from within.

I look at regrets, and errors
    And calculations run amuck
And wonder if tomorrow
    Might just have a little more luck.

I don't know – should I feel sorry
    Or cry in a bowl of tears –
But as I look back
And remember each day
    I did what I wanted –
And said what I had to say.

Maybe I'm right
    And maybe I'm wrong,
But I've always felt
With my wife at my side
    I stood a chance to win
And keep my pride.

And wish each and all
    Your Humpty Dumpty won't fall.

Six Feet Tall, Three Feet Short

HE SAID, YOU SAID, I SAID

But did I say, you said?
    Or did you think I said –
That tomorrow is another day.

It is you know,
    And will always be so –
A perfect chance to start over,
    And hope the day,
Won't end the way –
    That you said,
    I said,
That it would.

It could you know,
    "Cause I ought to know –
Since you said, I said I know
    So lets' hope it will be
Good for you – And
    Perfect for me.

Like you said I said –
    Or you think I said –
Tomorrow is another day.

And am I glad I said it!

    P.S.

He also said I said –
    I love being in love
With the Lady I love. –

Moses Bilsky

THE BEST

The best of the best –
        Is while talking
In the coveted nest
        Of midnight,
We built,
        In 54 years.

Its moment in time
        Is when not in rhyme,
We talk –
        Hold hands,
        And review all
        Secrets –
That the ceiling
        And walls
Have listened to
        Over the long haul
        Of marriage –
In its purest form.

What sayeth Fair Maiden.
        Tell me why we remain

Lovers – How come
        Through knocks
        And drops –
Which drown in tears,

        And –
Recover in laughter
        And hold on tight.
Then clasp each other,
        In complete awe.

Six Feet Tall, Three Feet Short

Lucky? It takes more
    Than commitment.
It's called trust –
    And courage
And desired truthfulness.
    With simulated prayers,
And the knowledge of
    "I can if you can"
Because: If you do –
    I do.
Together –
    Because it's called
Love –
    But it's really
Life –
    At it's Best.......

Dedicated To My Friend – Roslyn

Moses Bilsky

THAT'S IT

I want to walk the walk,
    And talk the talk –
And never the twain shall meet.
    For when the pain was gone,
And I could clearly see –
    Guess who won?
You can bet it was me.

When I look back now –
    Though it's hard to believe
It all was worth the while
    I struggled constantly –
To live –
    And beat the nightmares
Of defeat –
    While watching the clock
Turn minutes
    Into hours.
Thinking time had stood still
    As my piano
    Plays music –
    But I'm not there.

I'm counting pills.
    Blue ones,
    White ones,
    Oval and
    Square,
It's a serious game,
    Does anyone care?

Racing against time
    Left –
To share love,
    And thoughts,
Hoping tomorrow
    Remains today

Forever –
    Can it – ?
    Will it – ?
Why not –.
Accept whatever,
    It's all you've got.

AH! WHAT'S UP DOC?

Fleet conjures up the thought – NAVY –
    But such is not so in my case.
It's far more worrisome and intrusive,
    And borders on the edge of abusive.

When irregularity replaces regular –
    And the Doctor is but a telephone away,
His advise is a comfort of sort
    Especially when the Navy's in port.

Then off to the drugstore I go
    For the recommended portion I know
Easy to do – easy to use.
    Don't you believe it –
It's a bomb with a fuse.

So I'll wait – and I'll see –
    If the overall plan,
Can do what it can.
    To return me to normalcy.

I'm normal ? !

Are you dreaming ! ?

Moses Bilsky

ALL TOGETHER NOW

"Now picture this",
    I said to me,
Sitting 'neath –
    The willow tree.

Watching the tender green
    Rhythmically sway,
As in my mind,
    Musicians play.

The sad song
    Of wind and rain.
Covering up –
    The cry of pain.

Why my concern?
    I'm long past that –
I'm healthy now,
    And that's a fact.

But it's for you –
    I realize now,
That my strength, and courage,
    A path might plow.

And bring you comfort
    By wish and prayer –
That you come forth,
    From medical care.

And find the hope
    And happiness too –
That makes a painful day,
    Brand new.

So we can say –

Six Feet Tall, Three Feet Short

"All together now".
Prayer works
And that's a -
"WOW"

NIGHTMARES

Nightmares play with monsters –
    And linger, and stay awhile.
While Happy Dreams –
    On moonbeams slither
And fade away
    While you beg to differ.

Come on! Lend a smile
    And a little laugher too.
'Cause I'm running scared –
    And need a friend
That I can trust
    While on the mend.

It seems to me,
    That the more I look
The less I find
    On pages of the book –
Of LIFE –
    And stories
    That I might compare
    To now –
    And yesteryear.

Moses Bilsky

Sure we're tired –
    As the time slips by.
But the clock keeps ticking
    And we have things to do,
With promises to keep –
    There's no time to weep.
    Just do – just be,
    Expect, with fingers crossed
And hope the way
    Is seldom lost.

One more chance –
    One more try –
    Don't cry
    'Cause tears distort
From 20/20
And the goal,
    Is almost in sight.

A CRYING SMILE

I know it's early –
    So I hope I'm not late –
To tell you a story
    I have to relate.

About you – and me
    And the others around
Who think they're not touched
    By the aimless sound.

Of loneliness – and tears in the night
    And "What shall we do"
In our helpless plight
    I know it affects me
And I'm sure of you too.

Six Feet Tall, Three Feet Short

A stranger came up
    In the grocery aisle
And looked at us
    With a crying smile.

Would we please stop a moment
    We looked like we'd listen -
I'm in my cart, with my wife along side
    She needed advise –
Her tears of anguish, she couldn't hide.

She told us her story
    Of the trouble she's in
With uncontrollable tremors
    She begins to begin.

They're tears, - and laughter
    Hugs to us each –
About her in-laws – and strokes
    And rehab for old pokes.

Of fingers cramped, with fists made tight,
    Recovery not near – just a long health fight.
We don't know her name –
    Nor she, know ours
This carried on for an hour
    We finally pushed on
Leaving her shaking
    In the frozen food aisle.
Further down in the store
    When we could glance at each other
We agreed at once
    She needed a Mother. –

Not Us –

Moses Bilsky

WOW – AND THEN – WOW

I'm addicted to –
    Afrin –
    Fleet –
    Prunes –
    Chocolate –
    Love – And
    Life.

My genius done gone –
    And dried up.
And the drain
    Which once worked
Is now just a cup –
    Soupy, and cloudy
And sounding quite dowdy,
    It's no longer filled –
To the brim.

So if the Sky were full of rainbows
    And I had one last breath
To breathe –
    I'd draft as deep as possible
And freeze the breath –
How good life has always been
    Unbeknown to me –
And yet to be remembered
    By you.
The clouds drifting by,
    Hold a symbol of life –
Yet their shapes and forms
    Spell beauty
And questions for tomorrow-
    To be deciphered.

Six Feet Tall, Three Feet Short

When the morrow
    Arrives,
The moment once thought –
    Fades beyond recognition,
And we ask –
    Does time remain
To complete the purpose
    Of Life? –
To help –
To love
To create
    And to express thanks
For completing our
    Original purpose
Of having arrived
    To experience
The Why?

Moses Bilsky

Dear Don,   10/25/2009

So you made up your mind to leave the old playground, for loftier and holy places. Can't say that I blame you, as tired as you were, and how rested you now will be.

We'll miss you, but always reflect how lucky we all were for so many years of being blessed with your presence.

I for one, know you were the first person I met in Louisville when enrolled in Jr. High school way back in 1937 –
Others may not remember, but I do – about lots of things –
Napoleon Blvd. – I used to play your Mom's piano – she thought I was pretty good – Remember your first car – I loved the rumble seat, when we double dated. Isn't it strange that my wife – knew your wife as Benovitz and Fischer before they ever thought of us.

I played the piano wherever I could – AZA Dances – Linker played drums when the dance band took a break – he was good – Linker, Bornstein and Bilsky – what a long, valuable friendship. You at Speed Scientific, I at U of L law school – and I'm not sure where Bob went.

I do know the 3 of us knew how to pick Woman. Look at the wives we got lucky with – each with bragging rights in excess of 55 years to the same women.

Wow – we've been lucky, and come to think of it, so have they –

Well dear friend, I write this note at 4:00AM – two days after you chose to leave us. How lucky we are to have shared your time with us.

Good night, Good bye, thank you for being my friend for 72 years. And now, how lucky God is to have you in his realm.

Bye Bye –

Moe

Six Feet Tall, Three Feet Short

BAREFOOT BEGGAR

You've seen him –
    Did you see him glance?
No – because he doesn't.

Did you offer help?
    Just moved along,
And placed the scene –
    In your memory bank!

Bare dirty feet –
    Shuffling at drag pace
He never looks up
    He doesn't ask –
    No smile.

To busy keeping his feet
    On the cardboard
Instead of shoes.

Where's he coming from?
    Where's he going?
Where does he live?
    Where does he sleep?
How and where or what
    Does he eat?

Could you help?
    Yes –
Do you help?
No –

Thank God it's not me –
    Or you,
Or anyone I know
    I just wonder –
Why it is,
    What it is.

Moses Bilsky

And I don't understand
    The WHY of it all.

IT TAKES MORE THAN EFFORT

Did I scream all night –
    Did I cry all day?
Maybe I screamed all day,
    And cried all night.

Does it really matter?
    To whom?
Not to me – I can't hear it,
    Since it's so far remote
That its' irrevocable –
    And I wonder, as an author,
That someone else once wrote –
    For whom the bells toll?
They toll for me.

What kind of quality life
    Avails itself for me?
To share with
    My Wife – Family – Friends,
I must pretend contentment
    That this is my lot –
Six weeks
    The damnedest therapy
Imaginable. Prognosis –?
    Hope. Pray – fingers crossed
Something – Anything – Please God!

Six Feet Tall, Three Feet Short

DON'T EXPECT A MIRACLE

55 Years Wedded Bliss
    Were celebrated this night
After thinking the day
    Seemed to be going alright.

So we dressed after nap
    I put a snap in my cap
And out the door
    To watch the rain
Start to pour.

Reverse course, I said
    And the cart turned right
The wife near my shoulder
    We were off for the night

Hotel, and cocktails
    Near the fireplace warmth
Perfect, I thought –

And then the late at night
    We watched uptight
The old programs and junk,
    On TV with light.

They advertized this
    And they advertized that
Till a pain in the ass
    Was right where I sat.

TV bargains,
    Specials and all
Product and realty,
    Watch the prices fall.

Moses Bilsky

Until the hour went to sex
    Was the subject at hand
We couldn't believe
    Our life had been bland

So with 'Extenze' for each –
    We could turn life quite sour
Into a beautiful peach.

Wow – just think
    I could shape
With a quick dose
    A new shape.

WITH APOLOGY TO COLE PORTER

Maybe I is –
    And maybe I ain't.
But I know for certain
    I married a Saint.

"Cause
    I can't help
Lovin'
    That Gal o'mine.

She's on my left
    She's on my right
She's up with me
    In the middle of the night.

Gosh oh me
    How lucky
Can I be.

– BUT –

Six Feet Tall, Three Feet Short

I've got a problem
    Which I can't put aside
The telephone rang
    And there's no place to hide

Some how or other –
    One scream after another
Did not help the fact
    That my CANCER'S back
For a deadly attack.

To tired to fight
    With my mind in flight
It's nightmares and pain
    And no ground to gain.

But regardless of happenings
    And set backs for days
It's the fight of a lifetime –
    With courage, that pays.

– I'll Try –

Moses Bilsky

INVOLVED

Why – Oh Why
    Am I blind
In one eye – ?

And can't see,
    Out of the other?

Perhaps I don't
    Bother,
Or too lazy to care
    I'll go my way –
So no one will
    Stare.

Don't rock the boat
    It will swamp us –
For sure,
    And the difference
Will show us
    The wrong
From the pure.

The easy way
    Out
Is to just shout,
    "Don't bother me".

Six Feet Tall, Three Feet Short

JUST A THOUGHT ONE NIGHT

So I peed in the corner,
    And farted through the night.

And said it wasn't me –
    But my neighbor on the right,

It never hurts to lie
    And blame someone else,
As long as I can cry,
    And keep Vodka on the shelf.

I'll do the devil's dance
    And prance around quite drunk
Until I can't stand up –
    And smell like an old dead skunk.

As I waddle to my grave,
    With the end quite short and sweet –

I'll give a goodbye handshake,
    While I drink my Vodka Neat.

Moses Bilsky

DOING VS. THINKING

So tell me –
    What difference does it make,
If I lie awake
    While the moon fades
Beyond my sight.
    To the right
Into total darkness.

And I write –
    What I would, or might say
Should the occasion arise
    Tomorrow –
Or even the next day.

But now, is tonight
    And on my mind,
Is my plight
    To promise I will do,
What must be done –

To smile, to laugh, to help,
    To listen, to advise,
To try, to learn, to tolerate
    Be kind, hear music, see beauty –
Love all that I have.
And share with those who have not.

Six Feet Tall, Three Feet Short

WHEELCHAIR

Wheelchair – Wheelchair
    To what –
Does it compare?

To go – to stop
    Stay or move
Turn –
    Left, right
Circle.

Comfort
    Sometimes –
Sleep
    Sometimes –
Play
    Sometimes –
Cry
    Often
Pray
    Always
Lucky
    Better than the alternatives.

Restless
    Forever
Necessary
    In most cases
For me –
    Forever.
Deserving
    I don't think so
Forgiving
    Not really
But lucky to live
    Yes Sir –
Unexpected
    Emergency –

Moses Bilsky

Not really –
    But – Perhaps on the cutting edge
Of because and be safe –
    I dialed – 911
I told operator
    "Conscious" "Nothing unusual"
Just can't catch my breath.

Hello – How are you –
    Age, location etc, etc......
"Be right there"
    And they came –
6 Hefty's – able to lift mountains
    Or investigate rubble.

How lucky I was
    No cause for alarm –
They have all information available –
    Put Marcia in side seat
Ready – blast siren
    – GO –
And we went.

Wow – 12' x 8' area
    Dr.'s – Nurses – Students
And eyes peeking and poking
    Oxygen available, Feel better

Students & Nurses
    Looking for veins
Here a needle –
    There a needle
    Everywhere a needle prick,
    Veins on holiday
Can't find –

Don't touch me without my Dr's approval –
    He's on the phone.
Have checkup

Six Feet Tall, Three Feet Short

Since I'm already there.
    AM tests okay
Five hours later
    All's well – okay to Go home.

Except ER is a one-way in.
    On your own to get out.
No clothes, Send for Daughter
    Get wearable's – wheelchair
Push out to street
    On my own again!

Moses Bilsky

ALL'S WELL

Hokum –
Pokum –
Scallywag Yokum
    A friend of mine indeed.

Trust 'im –
Cheat 'im –
Find 'im or Beat 'im,
    He's never around if you need.

But borrow a buck –
    And pay back on time
Is all I ask
    Of any friend of mine.

However –
There are times I thrive on gossip
    And times I thrive on news –
And when I telephone family
    I hope for certain clues.

Dial I do – and ask of JAMIE
    What's new?
The answer is always
    Nothing –
Just checking in and
    What's new with me.

It all repeats for JORIE
    Who talks about seals and deals
And ends up with nothing –
    And what's new with me.

And then comes JEPH
    Which is usually shorter than the rest
Busy now – call you back
    Is all ok with me?

Six Feet Tall, Three Feet Short

So relate to wife –
   All's well with the three
She's at my side
   And all's well with me.

SATISFACTION

The end of a lifetime,
   Is far more difficult
Than you think.
   Since remembering each moment
Stretches from ballroom dance
   To the kitchen sink.

There are so many good times
   Mixed in with the bad –
That tears become torrents,
   And drown in the sad.

It's hard to admit,
   How lucky you are –
When you end up near ninety
   And can't drive the car.

And walking hurts –
   And is far to slow.
Especially when you feel,
   Like you're raring to go.

So you take your time,
   And sit in your chair
While someone pushes
   Who really does care.

And you see in eyes
   That hold tears and trust
So you know your safe,
   Come Hell, High-water, or Bust.

Moses Bilsky

Had I known the pitfalls
    Old age brings forth
And I have the same partner
    Who emits such warmth
I'd do it all over –
    For I've had the best,
And ended luckier
    Than all the rest.

So I'm content
And I hope she is too –
'Cause to train a stranger
    Would be out of the blue.

Six Feet Tall, Three Feet Short

LUCKY

In the year of Whomever
    Being Two-oh-oh-Two
I suffered a stroke
    Far worse than the Flu.

After a complete plastic Aorta –
    From some point thereon,
My health dropped out
    To where I don't walk
    To get about. – So,
With Cancer Times Seven –
    Hoping for good health in – '11

A fight – I did -
    I have –
    I will –
    I do –
        Colon – Back – Bladder
        Kidney – Bladder – Prostate
        Bladder, Again and again.

You don't want the details –
    I don't want to remember.
But I got home the other day –
    With prayers and hopes,
That I'm here to stay.

Moses Bilsky

IT'S DIFFERENT DOWN HERE

What's different –
    From where I sit
With tummies and fannies galore.
    Is you can't tell
Whose voices it is,
    When all you can see
Is the floor.

Notice too, that sounds –
    And actions –
Always come from behind.
    So that body; and sight
Is twisted enough
    Separate day from night.

It's peculiar though,
    That I have to ask –
My Wife,
    The who – and the what – and the where
And what's going on
    In the world above
To know if I really care.

So just for once, I wish
    I could carry a dish,
And completely
    Take care of myself.
So that I could at least
    Reach the top shelf.
And say –
    "Been There,
    Done That"
All by my little ole-self.

Six Feet Tall, Three Feet Short

Lean over – and look
    If I'm awake or a sleep
And count me an
Equal to you.

You'll be surprised
    I'm a likeable guy
Ready to go and do
    And may be just once
Really consider me
    As tall as you.

Moses Bilsky

SAFETY ABOUNDS

It's a sorrowful fact,
    That I'm coming back
To the end of my years.
    And because of same
Many are filled with tears.

It really makes no sense
    Since most all –
Are filled with happiness,
    And I am always surrounded
By love and care –
    Far more than I dare –
For which I pray.

What is it?
    That wrankles my brain,
And sets a course
    Towards stupidity of thought –
Of being alone
    In an hour of need,
For a comfort zone.

Try as I will,
    And shut my eyes tight,
The 'morrow will bring
    Love, safety – and light.

Manufactured By: RR Donnelley
Momence, IL USA
February, 2011